W9-AYB-217

# Social Security and
# Early Retirement

**CESifo Book Series**
Edited by Hans-Werner Sinn

*The Political Economy of Education: Implications for Growth and Inequality*, Mark Gradstein, Moshe Justman, and Volker Meier

*The Decline of the Welfare State: Demography and Globalization*, Assaf Razin and Efraim Sadka, in cooperation with Chang Woon Nam

*The European Central Bank: Credibility, Transparency, and Centralization*, Jakob de Haan, Sylvester C. W. Eijffinger, and Sandra Waller

*Alleviating Urban Traffic Congestion*, Richard Arnott, Tilmann Rave, and Ronnie Schöb

*Boom-Bust Cycles and Financial Liberalization*, Aaron Tornell and Frank Westermann

*Social Security and Early Retirement*, Robert Fenge and Pierre Pestieau

# Social Security and
# Early Retirement

Robert Fenge and Pierre
Pestieau

CESifo Book Series

The MIT Press
Cambridge, Massachusetts
London, England

© 2005 Massachusetts Institute of Technology

All rights reserved. No part of this book may be reproduced in any form by any electronic or mechanical means (including photocopying, recording, or information storage and retrieval) without permission in writing from the publisher.

MIT Press books may be purchased at special quantity discounts for business or sales promotional use. For information, please e-mail ⟨special_sales@mitpress.mit.edu⟩, or write to Special Sales Department, The MIT Press, 55 Hayward Street, Cambridge, MA 02142.

This book was set in Palatino on 3B2 by Asco Typesetters, Hong Kong. Printed and bound in the United States of America.

Library of Congress Cataloging-in-Publication Data

Fenge, Robert.
Social security and early retirement / Robert Fenge and Pierre Pestieau.
  p.  cm.—(CESifo book series)
Includes bibliographical references and index.
ISBN 0-262-06249-6 (hc : alk. paper)
1. Social security—European Union countries. 2. Early retirement—European Union countries. 3. Social security. 4. Early retirement. 5. Old age pensions—Finance.
I. Pestieau, Pierre, 1943–. II. Title. III. Series.
HD7164.5.F46   2006
368.4′3′0094—dc22                                                      2005047472

10  9  8  7  6  5  4  3  2  1

# Contents

# Series Foreword

This volume is part of the CESifo Book Series. Each book in the series aims to cover a topical policy issue in economics. The monographs reflect the research agenda of the Ifo Institute for Economic Research, and they are typically "tandem projects" where internationally renowned economists from the CESifo network cooperate with Ifo researchers. The monographs have been anonymously refereed and revised after being presented and discussed at several workshops hosted by the Ifo Institute.

# Preface

We have brought two different perspectives to this volume about early retirement. Pierre's interest in social security—particularly its redistributive aspects—goes back to the early 1980s. Robert has worked primarily on the efficiency aspects of the transition from pay-as-you-go to fully funded pension schemes. Our interest in the causes and the implications of early retirement is more recent and was triggered by the realization that European social security systems were being burdened by a declining effective retirement age. For example, Belgium, Pierre's home country, is known today not for having superb painters or highway lighting but for having the highest public debt and lowest effective age of retirement of all of the countries in the Organization for Economic Cooperation and Development. When we decided to examine this situation, we did not realize how difficult it would be to write about early retirement, even without reviewing the enormous amount of existing literature on the topic.

This book cannot be separated from Pierre's joint work with a number of coauthors whose friendship made the research stimulating. Among them are Robin Boadway, Helmuth Cremer, Maurice Marchand and Philippe Michel (whose premature death saddened us), Sergio Perelman, and Uri Possen. Pierre's work on the subject started with his involvement in the National Burean of Economic Research project on social secuaity and retirement around the world. He is indebted to all those who are involved in this ongoing project, particularly its leaders, Jon Gruber and David Wise.

Robert wishes to thank Sascha Becker for providing his statistical expertise. For providing facilities and helpful comments, he is also grateful to the Department of Economics at the University of Warwick, where he spent a sabbatical year in 2003 and 2004 writing some parts of the book.

We also would like to thank all the coresearchers whose efforts, direct or indirect, appear in this book: Georges Casamatta, Arnaud Dellis, Raphaël Desmet, Alain Jousten, Mathieu Lefèbvre, Jean-Marie Lozachmeur, Gwenaël Piaser. We thank Claudine Chmielewski for typing the manuscript and processing some of the tables and figures. Finally, we are grateful to CESIfo for providing a stimulating setting for writing this book and the four reviewers who made extremely helpful suggestions.

# Social Security and
# Early Retirement

# 1          Introduction

Among the most striking developments of the last forty years are the trends toward earlier retirement, higher longevity, and consequent growing length and cost of retirement. Over the last four decades, for example, longevity in the French labor force has increased by 6.6 years for men and 7.5 for women, and the effective age of retirement has declined by 5.3 years for men and 7.5 for women.

Economics does not have much to say about longevity. Even though increasing life expectancy is likely to be partly due to economic factors, many other noneconomic factors contribute to longer lifespans. In fact, the relationship between economics and longevity is not clearly understood.

But economics has a lot to say about the trend toward earlier retirement. One of the dominant factors driving this trend is the long-term increase in economic wealth, which permits workers to enjoy rising living standards even as they spend a growing percentage of their lives outside the workforce.

Other important factors that have contributed to earlier retirement are expanded retirement benefits and lowered eligibility ages. Assuming that workers look at future income streams from earnings and pensions when considering retirement, a significant increase in benefits in the last decades has reduced the incentive to postpone retirement. The increasing attractiveness and availability of pathways into retirement at earlier ages is one of the most striking explanations for the lower effective retirement age in most industrialized countries.

Another explanation that is frequently advanced for earlier retirement is that workers' health has declined while physical requirements for work have grown more rigorous. Although this explanation is one of the least persuasive ones, health does play a role in the timing of individual retirement decisions. But there is no convincing evidence that the health of 55- to 70-year-old workers declined over the period in which their labor-force participation was falling. Recent evidence about the physical disabilities of older people suggests, instead, that their health is improving. Regarding work onerousness, it seems that a much smaller percentage of today's jobs require strenuous physical effort.

For a majority of economists, the trends toward higher longevity, earlier retirement, and increased economic wealth are not only related to but also signs of improved welfare. Recent studies of economic growth incorporate leisure and longevity to correct for standard indicators of development. This evolution is perceived as regrettable only if we cannot afford it. But this is far from being certain. Even with optimistic growth forecast, most countries (particularly those with an early retirement age) will be unable to meet their pension obligations. Early retirement is costly. According to recent estimates, its current cost in countries that belong to the Organization for Economic Cooperation and Development (OECD) amounts to 7.1 percent of gross domestic product.[1]

This book examines various explanations for why early retirement has become such a burden for social security systems, tries to identify the most important determinants of this trend, and proposes some pension reforms that might help to reverse this trend. We believe that the strongest factors that are driving early retirement are the financial incentives provided by expanding social security systems. A comprehensive and powerful way to capture those financial incentives in one concept is the implicit tax involved in social security systems. We discuss this implicit tax from several perspectives. From a normative point of view, second-best policies need to minimize the distortions of labor-supply and retirement decisions that are caused by social security taxes on a payroll basis. This optimal-tax approach also includes an analysis of alternative sources for financing benefits, such as consumption and capital income taxation. From a positive point of view, policies are designed in a way that disencourages work among older persons, and the political economy of early retirement provides useful insights into how support for such policies arises and why it is difficult to reverse the trend toward early retirement.

In this study, we do not survey the vast research output dealing with retirement but instead focus on analyzing the labor supply. The expansion of social protection and, in some countries, the development of employer-sponsored pension plans induces workers to stop working early. The voluntary decisions of older workers to leave the labor force are based on the amount of income they can expect to receive when they leave the workforce. This income can come from standard pension programs, but also from other components of social protection such as disability insurance, unemployment insurance, and early retirement schemes that provide relatively generous benefits well before the normal retirement age (which is 65 in many countries). One reason to concentrate on labor supply is that we believe it is particularly relevant to European Union countries. We also think that it is the most interesting subject for economists concerned with issues of choice and responsibility. But labor-demand forces also drive older workers out of the labor force. Employers (and government) have been active in forcing older persons out of work, especially when earnings increase with seniority and exceed productivity. Employers who wish to cancel labor contracts with older workers may be backed by governments that hope to free jobs for young unemployed.

Chapter 2 deals with empirical evidence on early retirement. It shows how the pathways into retirement—such as old-age pension schemes, early retirement schemes, disability insurance, and unemployment insurance—are implemented into the social protection systems in different countries. We present the existing evidence on the decline in the workforce-participation rate of elderly workers and on their increasing longevity. A comparison of retirement patterns over time and between genders reveals that retirement age is sensitive to regulations of the social security system (such as changes in eligibility age). Furthermore, we find that health as a determinant of early retirement plays a minor role compared to financial incentives. Chapter 3 concentrates on how to measure such incentives that are imbedded in social security systems. It presents and evaluates different ways to measure those incentives, including accrual rates of social security wealth, the peak value, and the option value. Among other things, we give a number of estimates of implicit taxes on prolonged activity and show the relationship between these taxes and the retirement decision.

Introducing the theoretical part of the book, chapter 4 presents the model used in the book and some concepts pertaining to actuarial neutrality and fairness. It appears that for the retirement decision, what matters is marginal neutrality. The optimal payroll-tax rates of a pay-as-you-go (PAYG) pension scheme that are derived in this chapter minimize distortions of labor-supply and retirement decisions, and the question of whether distortions are smaller in a fully funded (FF) pension scheme is also discussed. In chapter 5, we turn to aspects of the political economy of early retirement. Here we address the question of why in some societies effective retirement is early and why reforms that are considered necessary and socially desirable face resistance.

Pensions schemes traditionally are built within the framework of an overlapping-generations model. The age of retirement is fixed, and the issue is to find the optimal scheme from the standpoint of a modified "golden rule." In chapter 6, we extend this model by allowing for an endogenous retirement age. In this framework, the problems of payroll taxes as a source for financing pensions are analyzed, and alternative ways of financing (such as consumption and capital income taxes) are discussed. One new result that we obtained from this growth model is that as people retire later, the level of capital accumulation turns out to be lower. In chapter 7, we turn to the issue of disability insurance, which often seems to be one of the normal routes to early retirement. The issue we are concerned with is that of sorting out those who are truly disabled and those who are mimicking disability because they are leisure prone. The tendency today is to cut disability insurance benefits to avoid having elderly workers use this route to exit the job market. We argue that the victims of such reforms would be those who are truly disabled. The same applies to unemployment insurance.

Chapter 8 is devoted to the demand side of the retirement decision. Some claim that most elderly workers do not have the choice of working longer. According to this view, early retirement results from choices made by employers with the support of government and even unions. We discuss two points. First, many European governments believe that by pushing elderly workers into retirement, they free jobs for the young unemployed. We show that this is not the case. The second point pertains to the gap between the salary and the productivity of elderly workers. When that gap is large, employers have a strong incentive to get rid of their older employees. We show that this must not be the case. In chapter 9, we draw conclusions from the results of the preceding chapters and discuss those issues that are crucial for policy reforms of the social security system.

# 2    Facts and Trends of Early Retirement

## 2.1  Labor-Force Status

During recent decades, a common development in many OECD countries has been the increasing number of older people retiring from the labor force. The evolution of the labor-force participation rates of men age 55 to 64 shown in figure 2.1 suggests a dramatic decline in the fraction of older people in selected OECD countries who supplied labor in the market from 1960 to 2000. In the 1960s, participation rates were above 80 percent in nearly all OECD countries, but since then rates have declined significantly in all countries except Japan. In the 1990s, participation rates were below 50 percent in Belgium, Finland, France, and the Netherlands. In all other countries considered here, the rates ranged between 55 and 75 percent in that time.

Another statistic that demonstrates a declining trend in the number of older workers in the labor force is the employment rate. The figures in table 2.1 give the percentage of males age 55 to 64 who are employed. In 1995 and 2000, in a number of countries, less than half of the male population at age 55 to 64 is working. Employment of older workers has fallen in all countries over the past few decades. Although this trend appears to have come to a halt in many countries in the second half of the 1990s, this could to some extent reflect favorable cyclical conditions during this period.

This downward trend in labor-market participation and in employment of older men may have several causes. First, the generosity and accessibility of social security benefits have been extended over time in most OECD countries. The replacement rates of social security provisions have been increased, and the eligibility ages for receiving such benefits have been decreased. But in most social security systems, benefits cannot be drawn before age 60. In addition, other financial sources

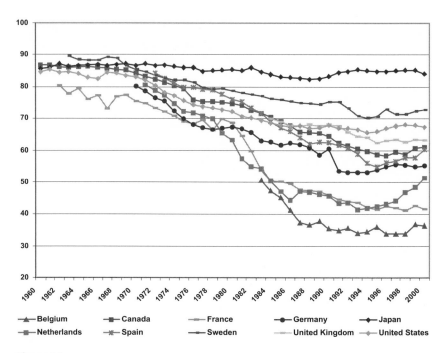

**Figure 2.1**
Labor-force participation rates of men age 55 to 64, 1960 to 2000
*Source: OECD Labor Market Statistics* (2001).

**Table 2.1**
Employment of male workers at age 55 to 64 as a percentage of male populations of the same age

|                | 1980 | 1990 | 1995 | 2000 |
|----------------|------|------|------|------|
| Belgium        | 47.7 | 34.3 | 34.5 | 35.1 |
| Canada         | 71.3 | 60.3 | 53.7 | 57.7 |
| France         | 65.3 | 43.0 | 38.4 | 38.5 |
| Germany        | 64.1 | 52.0 | 48.2 | 48.2 |
| Japan          | 82.2 | 80.4 | 80.8 | 78.4 |
| Netherlands    | 60.9 | 44.2 | 41.1 | 50.0 |
| Spain          | 71.5 | 57.2 | 48.4 | 55.2 |
| Sweden         | 77.5 | 74.4 | 64.4 | 67.8 |
| United Kingdom | 62.6 | 62.4 | 56.1 | 59.8 |
| United States  | 69.7 | 65.2 | 63.6 | 65.6 |

*Source: OECD Economic Outlook No. 72* (2002).

facilitate early retirement for persons younger than age 60. Those pathways into retirement are financed by unemployment-related transfer schemes, disability pensions, occupational pensions, or special early retirement schemes.

## 2.2  Pathways to Retirement

Older persons can pursue several ways out of the labor force. The predominant pathway allows people at a standard entitlement age to receive public old-age pensions if they satisfy conditions of service history or working time. In most countries, this standard age is 65 years for men and will be adjusted from 60 to 65 years for women over the next several years in Austria, Belgium, Germany, and the United Kingdom. Typically, a person who is eligible for an old-age pension can retire before the standard age if he or she accepts a reduction of pension (the reduction increases as the retirement age decreases). In Germany, for example, for each year of early retirement up to five years before age 65, benefits are reduced by 3.6 percent. In addition, there is a reducing effect from fewer service years because benefits increase with the number of years in which contributions have been paid. Thus, one pathway into retirement is the old-age pension scheme, which includes provisions for retirement at an earlier age than the standard one—provided that pensions are adjusted according to the earlier retirement.

Some countries exempt certain groups from a reduction in pension when they retire before the standard age or provide pensions for retirement before age 60. For example, females can retire early in Germany and in Greece without any reduction in old-age pensions. In Germany, the early retirement of females used to be possible at age 60 after 180 months of membership in the public pension scheme and more than 10 years of contributions after age 40. The age limit was increased gradually to reach age 65 in 2004. In Greece, mothers of minor or disabled children are entitled to receive a full pension at age 55 after 6,000 working days or 20 years of insurance. Conditional on years of insurance or employment, early retirement is possible in Belgium, Germany, Greece, Italy, Luxembourg, and Portugal. For example, Belgian males and females at the age of 60 are entitled to old-age pensions if they have been employed for 28 years, but the required period of employment will be increased to 35 years by 2005. In Italy, insured persons at age 55 and with a period of insurance of 35 years or, without an age limit, of 37 years used to be qualified to receive old-age pensions. Since 2002, though, limits have been increased to age 57 with 35 years of insurance or to 40 years of insurance without an age requirement. In the southern European countries, early retirement is possible but is conditional on heavy work or poor health. In Spain, workers in heavy manual labor or in unhealthy labor may retire early before attaining age 65. In Italy, early retirement is possible for employees who entered the working force early and paid contributions for more than 52 weeks at age 14 to 19. Workers doing heavy manual labor or having jobs with continuously changing workplaces are also entitled. And in Portugal, early retirement is possible at age 55 for persons exposed to heavy manual work or unhealthy activities. In some countries, early retirement is also allowed conditional on unemployment or difficult economic situations. In Italy, persons who work in enterprises that are in economic difficulties can be retired five years before the normal retirement age. In Portugal, unemployed persons are able to retire at age 60. If they were unemployed from the age of 50 and if 20 years of insurance are fulfilled, early retirement is possible at 55. In this case, pensions are reduced.

In addition to such early retirement schemes for old-age pensions, most countries provide disability pensions for incapacitated persons who are younger than the standard retirement age. Those pensions are paid to insured persons who are disabled and suffer from a substantial loss in their earning capacity. For example, in Belgium, Germany, Italy, and the Netherlands, insured persons who claim disability pensions have to pass earnings tests confirming that their earnings capacity is reduced below a certain minimum-earnings threshold. For persons who are eligible for disability pensions, this is another way to retire early and to achieve benefits in cases where other early retirement options are not available.

Other possibilities for leaving the labor force before the normal age of entitlement for pensions include unemployment benefits for elderly unemployed persons.

The labor-force status of German men and women in 2000 is shown in figure 2.2. This figure shows that the number of persons receiving public pensions increases dramatically at age 60 and after. While the number of employed persons decreases gradually around age 50, the fraction of pensioners—including persons receiving disability pensions—and the fraction of unemployed persons increases from that age. The share of registered unemployed persons rises to around 20

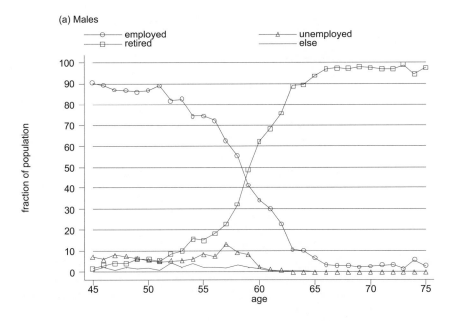

(a) Males

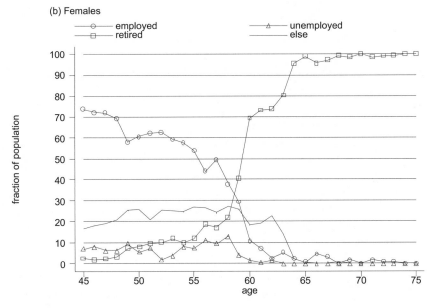

(b) Females

**Figure 2.2**
Labor-force status, Germany, 2000
*Source:* German Socio-Economic Panel (GSOEP) (2001). See Burkhauser (1991) for an English description, code books, and links to an internationally accessible GSOEP version.
*Note:* Employed = working; Unemployed = registered unemployed but willing to work; Retired = receiving public pensions, including old-age and disability pensions; Else = unofficially unemployed, housekeeping, vocational training.

percent of men and women before the age of 60. Unemployment is one of the many pathways to early retirement and (as is explained below) has been encouraged by the German government in preretirement schemes.

In many countries, official and unofficial compensation schemes exist for older unemployed persons. These schemes allow people to retire before they reach the entitlement age of early retirement schemes in pension systems. For example, in Germany, transfer payments for the unemployed enable labor-force exit before age 60. Figure 2.3 combines the status of retirement with the receipt of public pensions and pre-retirement compensations. After age 55, an increasing number of persons have retired without receiving public pensions (old-age or dis-ability). These are workers who receive unemployment compensation or severance pay from their former employer or both. Between age 55 and 60, up to 18 percent of men and about 10 percent of women use this way of preretirement. About 39 percent of all retired men receive such preretirement compensation at age 58, while about 61 percent retire because of disability. After age 65, all preretirees receive a public pension. The combination of severance pay and unemployment compensation is negotiable between workers and employers. These preretirement compensations are an unofficial way to induce early re-tirement by paying the worker the difference between their last salary and the unemployment benefit. These negotiations depend solely on the so-called social plan agreed on by a firm and their employees. The social plan organizes the dismissal of employees.

In addition, early retirement in Germany has been made possible by a public preretirement scheme. This scheme grants a subsidy to the employer and is paid by unemployment insurance if a younger worker is hired in place of a preretired worker. But this official preretirement scheme has not often been used by employers, while the unofficial severance pay plus unemployment benefits has been used more fre-quently to retire older workers early.

Institutional arrangements for early retirement have led to an in-creasing number of employees using one of those pathways into retire-ment before the standard age of entitlement. Figure 2.4 shows the sharp increase in the number of German pensioners from 1960 to 2000. Among all persons age 60 and older, 90 percent received a public pen-sion in 2000, while this share was 56 percent in 1960. A separation of the three types of public pensions shows that this rise was driven by the increasing share of recipients of old-age pensions from 22 to 60

(a) Males

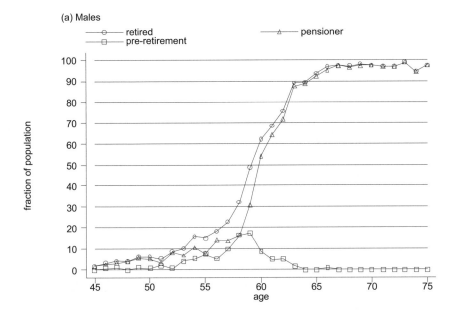

(b) Females

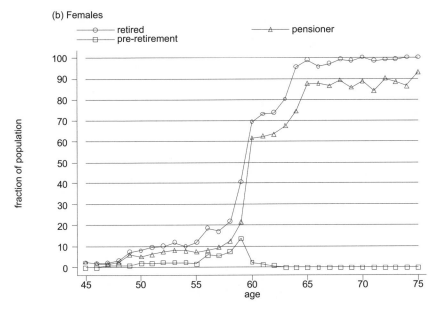

**Figure 2.3**
Public pensions and preretirement compensations, Germany, 2000
*Source:* GSOEP (2001).
*Note:* Pensioners = nonworking persons receiving old-age or disability pensions; Preretirement = nonworking persons receiving unemployment benefits or compensating payments as severance pay from a former employer.

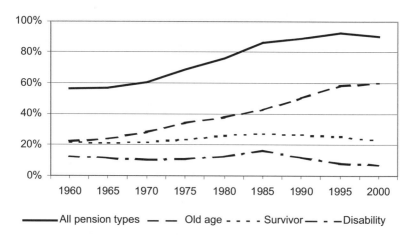

**Figure 2.4**
Share of persons age 60 or older receiving pensions, Germany, 1960 to 2000
*Source:* VDR (2002); Statistisches Bundesamt (2002).

percent. In 1972, when this rise began, early retirement benefits for female, unemployed, and older disabled workers were introduced in the old-age pension system. Beneficiaries of disability pensions rose in the early 1980s but decreased afterward due to stricter requirements. The share of survivor pensions remained rather constant.

## 2.3   Effective Retirement Age

After the 1972 introduction of early retirement schemes in Germany, the average age at first receipt of old-age pensions, which had been holding rather steady at age 65, began to decrease. Figure 2.5 shows that the average age of men when they first received a pension fell to 62 by the end of the 1990s. The average age of men who received disability pensions increased from 56 to 58 until 1972 and decreased to 52 in 2000. Taking these pension types together, the effective average retirement age for men who received public pensions has been far below the normal retirement age, which increased to 62 during economically prosperous decades in Germany and then decreased rapidly due to tighter labor-market conditions from 1973 to 1981. The average retirement age increased to age 59.8 in 2000.

The impact of the regulations of pension systems on the effective retirement age is perfectly reflected in the distribution of the ages at which workers receive a public pension (old-age or disability pension)

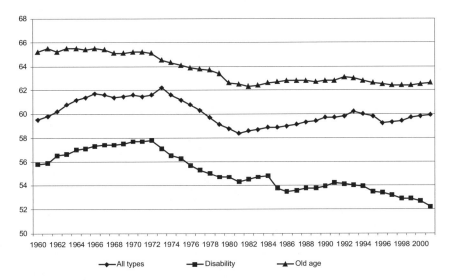

**Figure 2.5**
Average age at first receipt of public pensions, males, Germany, 1960 to 2000
*Source:* VDR (2002).
*Note:* The effective retirement age for a special pension type or for all types is calculated as the average of ages of persons having received the pension of a special type or of any type in the relevant year for the first time.

for the first time. Figure 2.6 shows clearly the change in the frequency of retirement ages of males across the decades in Germany. Most new male retirees enter the German pension system at three ages: 60, 63, and 65. This bundling can be related to the institutional ages of entitlement to old-age pensions—age 60 for males who are unemployed or disabled and age 63 for males with a long service history.[1] These flexible early retirement ages were introduced in 1972. The nearly general retirement age in 1970 was 65, and from that date until 2000 a substantial shift from age 65 to the earlier ages can be observed. By 1980, more new male retirees retired at age 60 than at 63 or 65. In 2000, a large retirement concentration at age 60 is evident. Thus, most new entries into retirement have used the opportunities for early retirement provided by the public pension system.

The impact of eligibility ages on retirement behavior can also be seen in the differences between men and women. Figure 2.7 shows the distribution of retirement ages for men and women under the German social security system in 2000. For both groups, there is a concentration of retirement at the standard retirement age of 65. Men and women

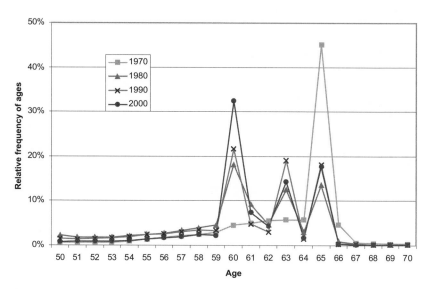

**Figure 2.6**
Distribution of retirement ages, males, Germany, 1970, 1980, 1990, and 2000
*Source:* VDR (1970, 1980, 1990, 2000).

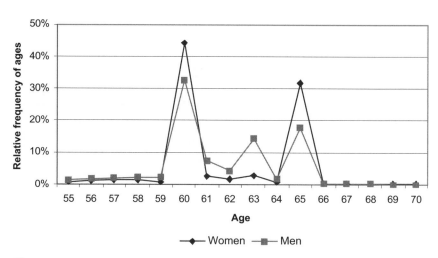

**Figure 2.7**
Distribution of retirement ages, males and females, Germany, 2000
*Source:* VDR (2000).

**Table 2.2**
Longevity and retirement age, 1960 to 1995

| | Men | | | | Women | | | |
|---|---|---|---|---|---|---|---|---|
| | Life Expectancy | | Retirement | | Life Expectancy | | Retirement | |
| | 1960–1965 | 1995–2000 | 1960 | 1995 | 1960–1965 | 1995–2000 | 1960 | 1995 |
| Belgium | 67.9 | 73.8 | 63.3 | 57.6 | 73.9 | 80.6 | 60.8 | 54.1 |
| France | 67.6 | 74.2 | 64.5 | 59.2 | 74.5 | 82.0 | 65.8 | 58.3 |
| Germany | 67.4 | 73.9 | 65.2 | 60.5 | 72.9 | 80.2 | 62.3 | 58.4 |
| Ireland | 68.4 | 73.6 | 68.1 | 63.4 | 72.3 | 79.2 | 70.8 | 60.1 |
| Italy | 67.4 | 75.0 | 64.5 | 60.6 | 72.6 | 81.2 | 62.0 | 57.2 |
| Spain | 67.9 | 74.5 | 67.9 | 61.4 | 72.7 | 81.5 | 68.0 | 58.9 |
| Sweden | 71.6 | 76.3 | 66.0 | 63.3 | 75.6 | 80.8 | 63.4 | 62.1 |
| United Kingdom | 67.9 | 74.5 | 66.2 | 62.7 | 73.8 | 79.8 | 62.7 | 59.7 |

*Source:* Cremer and Pestieau (2003).

also retire in large numbers at age 60 but for different reasons. This age is the early retirement age for women. The concentration of men retiring at that age is due to the eligibilty for old-age, disability, and unemployment benefits for older persons. The interesting feature of this figure is retirement behavior at age 63. At this age, a male worker is eligible to receive full pension benefits if he has a long service history. Because this option is not available for women, there is no concentration of women retiring at age 63. Thus, we can conclude that retirement is strongly influenced by social security regulations.

## 2.4  The Gap between Longevity and Retirement

While people are retiring earlier in most industrialized countries, the population is aging. One determinant of aging is increasing longevity. Table 2.2 shows the increasing gap between earlier retirement and longer life expectancy at birth from 1960 to 1995. The most dramatic widening of this gap can be observed in Spain. While life expectancy of men increased by 6.6 years, the retirement age of men decreased by 6.5 years. The difference between the expected end of life and the average retirement age for Spanish females increased by 17.9 years: life expectancy rose by 8.8 years, and retirement age decreased by 9.1 years.

The remaining time of life after retirement increased even more over recent decades if we take into account that life expectancy at the age of retirement is longer than life expectancy at birth. Figure 2.8 presents

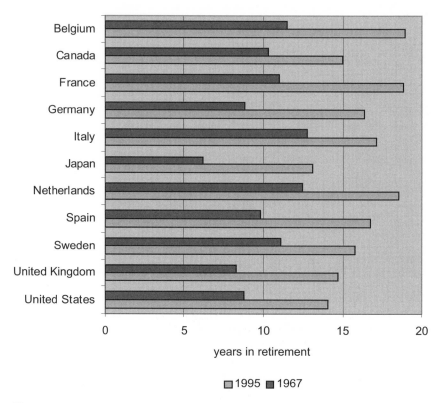

years in retirement

□ 1995  ■ 1967

**Figure 2.8**
Years in retirement of males, 1967 and 1995
*Source:* Blöndal and Scarpetta (1998b).
*Note:* Years in retirement = difference between the life expectancy for males age 55 and their average retirement age.

the difference of the life expectancy at age 55 and the effective retirement age of men in the years 1967 and 1995. This difference can be roughly interpreted as the average number of years in retirement. In nearly all OECD countries, the residual lifespan in retirement has increased by more than 30 percent. For example, in France the expected residual lifetime at age 55 increased from 19.5 to 22.9 years, while the effective retirement age decreased from 63.5 to 59.2 years in that period.

Figure 2.9 shows the continuously increasing average duration of receipt of public pensions (including old-age and disability pensions) in Germany. In 1960, a man received a public pension for 9.6 years on average, and this period of receiving public pensions increased to 14

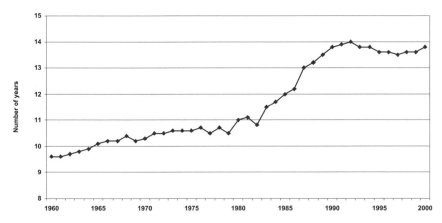

**Figure 2.9**
Average duration of receipt of public pensions for males (in years), Germany, 1960 to 2000
*Source:* VDR (2002).

years by 1992. Due to pension reforms that took place in 1992 and imposed stricter requirements for access to early retirement, the average duration for pension receipt decreased slightly in the late 1990s and was 13.8 years in 2000.

The increasing gap between life expectancy and retirement age can also be illustrated by comparing the average ages of the first and the last receipts of old-age pensions in Germany. Figure 2.10 shows the development of effective ages at which insured persons enter and leave the status of old-age pension recipients. While for men the period of receiving pensions increased from about 4 to 10 years, women experienced an increase from 4 to 16 years.

## 2.5   Health

The discussion about reasons for the rapid decrease in the labor-force participation of the elderly in recent decades provides two major competing conjectures. One argument claims that the financial incentives of the social security system induce older workers to withdraw from the labor force. Another argument suggests that the social security system plays a minor role and that the major reason for retirement is poor health in old age. Resolution of this debate is important for the development of retirement policy. In particular, if health is the primary factor, reductions in pre-65 retirement benefits would have little effect on

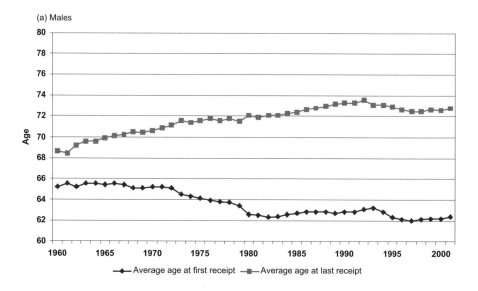

(a) Males

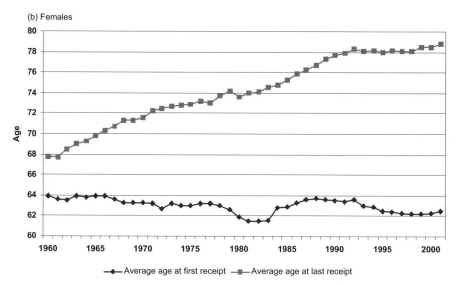

(b) Females

**Figure 2.10**
Average age at first and last receipt of old-age pensions, Germany, 1960 to 2000
*Source:* VDR (2002).

the labor-supply decisions of older workers but would instead lower the retirement income of those in poor health. Before investigating the financial incentives for early retirement in some detail in the next chapter, we examine the argument that poor health accounts for the significant increase in early retirement in the past 30 years.

Studies done in the late 1970s found that poor health is the primary consideration in early retirement decisions and that eligibilty for and benefits of the social security system are significant but less relevant determinants (Quinn, 1977; Boskin and Hurd, 1978). Those studies measured health status by responses to the question "Do you have a health condition that limits the kind or amount of work you can do?" Myers (1982, 1983) and others have criticized the use of those self-reported health measures. A major concern is that poor health may represent one of the few socially acceptable reasons for a person to be out of work. Therefore, a so-called justification bias may result in an interview where retired individuals cite health problems as the reason for their retirement instead of less acceptable reasons. Furthermore, some early retirement benefits are often available only for those deemed incapable of work. Thus, there may be a financial incentive to claim themselves retired due to poor health.

In response to this criticism, researchers have used more objective measures of health, such as information about specific health conditions or limitations, doctors' reports, or mortality rates. Parsons (1982) uses mortality as a measure for health and estimates a strong work disincentive effect of the social security replacement ratio, an effect not emerging when self-rated health is used as the health index. Anderson and Burkhauser (1985) measure a much stronger effect of financial variables like the wage rate when mortality instead of self-reported health is used. They find themselves persuaded that self-reports of health are "unsatisfactory measures because they can be affected by the availability and generosity of government-provided health and retirement benefits" (p. 324). Bazzoli (1985) compares preretirement and postretirement self-reports of health and concludes that individuals justify their retirement by claiming poor health. His results suggest that economic factors rather than health play the major role in retirement decisions.

To circumvent the health-measurement problem involving self-assessment, Boskin (1977) and Burkhauser (1979) used health variables that depend on total hours of illness in a given year. In several specifications, Boskin estimated that the health effect is not significant.

Although some workers undoubtedly retired for reasons of poor health, the data provided no support for the conjecture that poor health was the prime mover in retirement. Burkhauser found a significant effect of health on retirement decisions but emphasizes that even among those in poor health, changes in the value of their pensions and their earnings remain important.

Following this example, we use information from the German Socio-Economic Panel (GSOEP) (started in 1984) about the period of illness in the year preceding retirement. If health were the main reason for retirement, we should observe an increasing number of persons in bad health at their retirement age. Persons who decide to retire for health reasons would be characterized by being ill for a longer period during their last year of employment. Figure 2.11 presents the fraction of persons who retired in 2000 in Germany, and it shows among those persons the fraction who worked in the previous year and were sick for more or less than six weeks. Although the data show that men and women at age 60 to 65 seem to be sick at a higher rate before their retirement, they are only occasionally ill and not for longer than six weeks. There is no indication that a higher fraction of persons around retirement age were ill for a longer period in the year before retirement. Thus, we find no indication for bad health as a primary reason for retirement.

In the debate about self-reported versus objective measures of health, Bound (1991) concludes that self-reported measures lead to results in which health plays a larger role and economic factors a smaller role in retirement decisions than when more objective measures are used. Recent studies come to the same conclusion. In dynamic models of retirement behavior, those papers consider a variety of exit routes from employment and investigate the effects of different health measures and financial incentives. Bound, Schoenbaum, Stinebrickner, and Waidmann (1999) analyze the effects of self-reported health on alternative labor-force transitions like labor-force exit, job change, and application for disability insurance. They find that poor health is an important motive for older workers to withdraw from the labor force. Among all people in poor health, more than half of those who exit the labor force apply for disability insurance benefits. Kerkhofs, Lindeboom, and Theeuwes (1999) compare financial incentives with health motives for retirement decisions. In their dynamic framework, they analyze the effects of health (measured by both subjective and objective measures), eligibilty conditions, and replacement rates of alternative

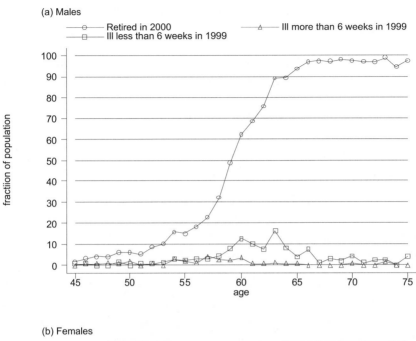

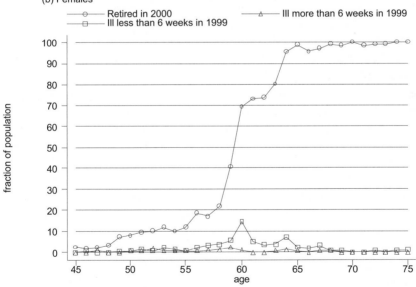

**Figure 2.11**
Health status before retirement, Germany, 2000
*Source:* GSOEP (2001).

exit routes from the labor force. They find that health matters but that the size of the effect depends crucially on the health measure used. Comparing the relative importance of financial incentives and health, they conclude that health is dominant in explaining transitions from labor into disability insurance schemes, while financial incentives are the most important determinant in the choice to apply for an early retirement scheme. The estimated effects of the financial incentives are robust to the alternative specifications of the health variable. Furthermore, they find evidence that income streams in alternative exit routes are compared in the retirement decision and that alternative exit routes act as substitutes.

The debate about the size of the health effect on retirement decisions has not been settled definitively. Poor health is one important reason for early retirement, but the extent of this effect depends a lot on the way that health is measured. There seem to be good reasons to rely more on objective than self-reported measures. And estimations using these objective measures tend to assign health a less important role than financial incentives in retirement decisions. But it also must be conceded that objective health measures (such as mortality or total hours of illness in the year before retirement) are rough proxies for the capacity to work. Hence, further research in testing more appropriate objective health measures for this purpose is needed. Recent results show also that it is important to differentiate the health effects of alternative routes to early retirement. For example, the exit route via disability insurance is surely one where health motives play a major role. Therefore, the incentives in such schemes need to be analyzed to sort out individuals with poor health from individuals who mimic such health problems but have other reasons to retire early. These issues are treated in chapter 7. The matter seems to be different in other early retirement schemes where health plays no significant role. Here the analysis is focused on the financial incentives of the social security schemes. How these incentives can be measured is the topic of the next chapter.

# 3    Implicit Taxation on Postponing Retirement

## 3.1  Single-Year Accruals

Social security systems establish strong incentives for the retirement decisions of older workers. Retirement decisions are affected by the change of social security wealth when work continues. Incentives to retire due to changes in social security wealth can be measured in several ways. One measure considers the one-year accruals of social security wealth.

Social security wealth is defined as the present value of the difference between future pension benefits and future contribution payments. Social security wealth may also include unemployment and disability benefits. The easiest way to measure the incentive effect is to calculate the gain or loss of social security wealth if a worker considers delaying retirement for one year. Then the worker has to weigh the additional wage income of this year against changes in social security wealth, and faces three effects on social security wealth. For this year, the worker would continue to pay contributions and would forgo benefits, and in future retirement years, he or she would have increased pension claims. If this increase in future benefits is high enough to offset the loss of benefits and the ongoing contribution payments during the additional year of working, then social security wealth does not change, and the system is neutral with respect to retirement decisions. If the higher future pensions do not compensate for the loss of pension and the ongoing contribution payments in one further year of employment, then social security wealth decreases. Hence, the gain in wage earnings is partially offset by a loss in social security wealth. The ratio of this loss to wage earnings is called the *social security implicit tax on earnings*. This tax distorts the decision to continue working and gives an incentive to retire early.

In most OECD countries, this is the case. Workers face a loss in social security wealth when they continue to work. The following calculations are used to quantify these effects in the case of Germany. The social security wealth of a worker who is $A$ years old and intends to retire at age $R$ is computed by

$$SSW_A(R) = \sum_{t=R}^{T} BEN_t(R) \cdot (1+r)^{-(t-A)} - \sum_{t=A}^{R-1} CON_t \cdot (1+r)^{-(t-A)},$$

where $SSW$ denotes social security wealth, $BEN_t(R)$ are the benefits at age $t$ that depend on the retirement age $R$, $CON_t$ denotes the contributions at age $t$, $1+r$ is the discount factor, and $T$ denotes the expected end of life. For simplicity, the probabilities of being alive to collect the future net benefits have been suppressed.

If a worker at age $A$ decides to retire not at age $R$ but at age $R+1$, then his social security wealth increases or decreases according to the different effects discussed above. The accrual rate of social security wealth $ACCR$ is defined as

$$ACCR_A(R+1) = \frac{SSW_A(R+1) - SSW_A(R)}{SSW_A(R)}.$$

If postponing retirement from age $R$ to age $R+1$ decreases the social security wealth, then the effective implicit tax rate on net wage earnings $IMPTAX$ can be calculated as

$$IMPTAX(R+1) = -\frac{SSW_A(R+1) - SSW_A(R)}{LABIN_R^{NET}},$$

where $LABIN_R^{NET}$ denotes the net labor income that the worker would earn if he or she worked at age $R$ and retired at age $R+1$.

Let us consider a German worker who was born in 1945. In 1965, he started to work and to pay contributions into the public pension system. For the ease of exposition, we restrict social security wealth to consist of only old-age pension benefits. In each year of his earnings history, the worker earned the yearly average gross wage income. In 2000, he reached age 55 and had to decide whether to leave the labor force or to continue working for one year. We assume that the worker lives until age 80. Figure 3.1 shows the accrual rates of social security wealth. Before age 60, the worker is not eligible for public pension benefits. Working a year longer until age 56 yields a pension that is one-thirty-fifth higher. At the same time, it implies a further year of

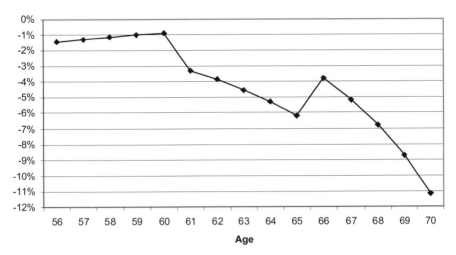

**Figure 3.1**
Accrual rates of social security wealth when retiring one year later, Germany, 2000
*Note:* The calculations are based on the CESifo pension model. For a closer description, see Fenge and Werding (2004). The calculations take into account the phasing in of the 2002 pension reform, which changed the adjustment of pensions to gross wage income. The average gross wage earnings from 2003 through 2030 are assumed to grow at 1.75 percent. For computations of the net wage earnings, the present rate of taxes and contributions are kept constant: average tax rate = 16 percent; contribution rate of public health insurance = 13.6 percent; contribution rate of public nursing insurance = 1.7 percent; contribution rate of unemployment insurance = 6.5 percent.

contributions. The net effect is a 1.4 percent decrease in social security wealth. Up to age 60, each additional year of working results in a negative accrual rate of about 1 percent. At age 60, the worker becomes eligible for public pensions, which are reduced to 82 percent of those pensions received at the standard age of entitlement—65. Postponing retirement for one year increases social security wealth due to higher future benefits (3.6 percent) and due to a longer service history. However, this is more than offset by a further year of contribution payments and forgone benefits. Social security wealth declines by 3.3 percent. In the following years until age 65, losses in social secruity wealth increase. After age 65, future benefits are increased by 6 pecent for each year of postponement. This reduces the loss in social security wealth significantly. However, after age 66, accrual rates decline further because the extra charge of 6 percent to future pensions is still too low to compensate for the effect of paying further contributions and losing pension income by working additional years.

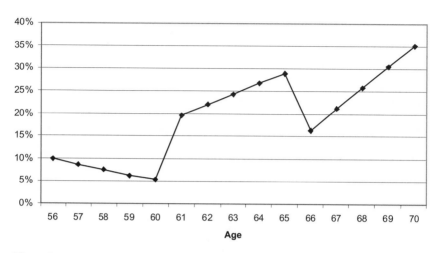

**Figure 3.2**
Implicit tax rate on continued work, Germany, 2000
*Note:* For assumptions underlying the calculation, see figure 3.1.

In figure 3.2, the accrual of social security wealth by postponing retirement is related to the average net wage income of the worker. If he
decides to postpone retirement by one year and to earn the average net
wage income, then he has to take into account that his social security
wealth decreases. Thus, the gain in wage earnings is partially offset by
a loss in future social security wealth. The ratio of this loss to net wage
earnings is defined as the social security implicit tax on earnings. In the
German case in 2000, the tax rates on earnings are relatively high and
reach 30 percent when the worker postpones retirement from age 64 to
65 or from age 68 to 69. Tax rates are even positive before age 60, when
the worker is not entitled to receive pensions if he retires. The reason
for this is that the increase in future pensions does not compensate
paying further contributions if the worker postpones retirement.

In many countries, the implicit tax rate can reach 80 percent or more
at some ages. Following Gruber and Wise (1999b), we define the *tax
force to retire* as the sum of the implicit tax rates on continued work,
beginning with the early retirement age and running through age 69.
Figure 3.3 presents the tax force for different OECD countries. The
average tax force across all countries is 4.6.

The relationship between the logarithm of tax force to retire and
the average effective retirement age in 11 OECD countries is shown in
figure 3.4. In countries with a higher tax force, the retirement age tends

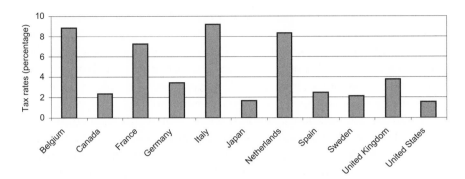

**Figure 3.3**
Tax force to retire
*Source:* Gruber and Wise (1999b).
*Note:* Sum of tax rates from early retirement age to 69. In the case of Germany, the implicit tax rates of an average earner age 55 in 1985 are used to compute the tax force.

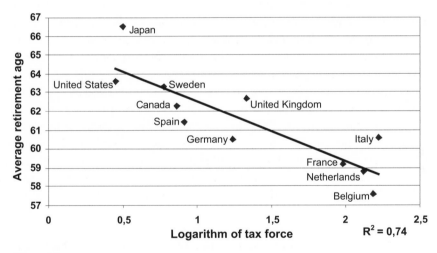

**Figure 3.4**
The relationship between average retirement age and tax force
*Source:* Gruber and Wise (1999a).
*Note:* Tax force = sum of implicit tax rates from early retirement age to age 69. Average effective retirement age in 1995.

to be lower. The solid line illustrates a regression of the average age on the logarithm of the tax force. About 74 percent of the variation in the average ages across countries can be explained by the tax force to retire. This suggests that nonneutral social security systems with respect to retirement decisions induce effectively early retirement.

One implication of the withdrawal of older men from the workforce is the forgone productive capacity of older employees. The proportion of men withdrawing from the labor force in a given age group can be measured by the area above the labor-force participation curve. Thus, the unused productive capacity at a certain age is defined as one minus the rate of labor-force participation at that age. Adding the unused capacity over all ages of a given age group measures the area above the labor-force participation curve in the range of those ages. Dividing the size of this area by the total area of the figure yields a measure of the unused capacity over the age range as a percentage of the total labor-force capacity in that age range. In figure 3.5, the unused capacity of the age group 55 to 65 is plotted against the tax force to retire. There is a strong relation between the tax incentives of social security

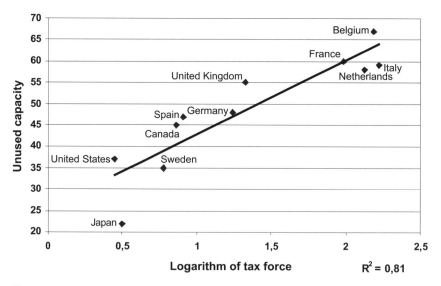

**Figure 3.5**
The relationship between unused capacity and tax force
*Source:* Gruber and Wise (1999a).
*Note:* Tax force = sum of implicit tax rates from early retirement age to age 69. Unused capacity = $(\sum_{age=55}^{65}(1 - LFPrate(age)))/10$.

systems and the forgone productive capacity of older employees. The proportion of men age 55 to 65 who have withdrawn from the labor force tends to increase significantly in countries with a higher tax force. The regression line shows that 81 percent of the variation of the unused capacity can be explained by the tax force to retire. Thus, the social security system creates strong incentives for workers in older ages to leave the labor force.

In a somewhat broader sense, Herbertsson and Orszag (2003) have calculated the burdens of early retirement, including economic costs of low labor-market participation of older workers such as lost output, benefit payments, and a lower tax base. They find that the costs associated with early retirement will rise considerably in the next years from 7.6 percent of output in 2003 to 9.1 percent of output in 2010. This rise is larger than the rise in the costs of early retirement over the 20 years from 1982 to 2003.

Calculations of the change of social security wealth indicate that financial gains from continuing to work may vary from year to year. In some social security systems, this may imply that working for one more year yields a small loss in the first year but that working a second additional year generates a large gain. In this case, a decision to retire that is based on the loss of social security wealth only in the next year would not take into account any large gains that are earned by working a second additional year. If those gains overcompensate the loss in the first year in present values, a decision looking forward only one year would forgo the gain that is earned by continuing to work for two years. Hence, retirement decisions taking into account only single-year accruals may be myopic decision rules. In the following section, decision principles are discussed that consider pension accruals not only in the next year but for several years in the future.

## 3.2 Peak-Value Approach

The peak-value approach addresses the fact that social security wealth attains in many cases a local maximum that is not a global maximum. Peak value, and not single-year accrual, allows the global maximum to be identified. Assuming that social security wealth assumes a global maximum at retirement age $R^*$, we can take this peak value as a benchmark for retirement decisions. This approach was proposed by Coile and Gruber (2000a, 2000b). It implies that a worker at age $A$ who considers retiring at age $R$ would have to compare the accumulation of social security wealth for both retirement ages:

$$PV_A(R^*) = SSW_A(R^*) - SSW_A(R).$$

By definition, $PV_A(R^*)$ is either positive or zero. If $PV_A(R^*)$ is positive, then the worker decides to retire at age $R^*$, which may be before or after age $R$. If $PV_A(R^*)$ is zero, then retirement age $R$ coincides with age $R^*$ at which the social security is maximal. Hence, the worker retires at age $R$.

For Germany, the calculations above demonstrate that social security wealth decreases at each retirement year after age 55 (see figure 3.1). Thus, maximal social security wealth is attained at the retirement age of 55. This example shows that the two principles (either the single-year accrual approach or the peak-value approach) lead to the same retirement decision if the accrual rates of social security wealth are negative at all possible retirement ages after the age of decision. In this case, the earliest possible retirement age maximizes social security wealth and will be chosen.

Gruber and Wise (1999a) calculate social security wealth and accrual rates at different retirement ages for several OECD countries. Table 3.1 presents some typical examples of the evolution of social security wealth. It shows that the decision principles regarding single-year accruals or the peak value of wealth lead in most countries to the same results. As in Germany, social security wealth in Italy decreases with a retirement age higher than age 55. This age turns out to be the optimal retirement age according to both decision rules. The same holds with social security systems in other countries, like Sweden and the United Kingdom.[1] In France, social security wealth increases if the worker decides to work until age 57. Retiring at age 58 would be optimal if the worker took into account the positive single-year accruals in the first years and the maximum of social security wealth at that age. Again, both incentive principles predict the same retirement behavior. The same pattern of accrual rates arises in countries like Belgium and Japan, where persons using either decision rule would retire at age 60.[2]

In some other countries, the social security system generates a wealth that decreases in the first years of retirement after age 54, then increases in a couple of years, and finally declines again. In the Netherlands, a worker at age 54 faces a loss in social security wealth if he or she decides to work for an additional year. The principle of single-year

**Table 3.1**
Social security wealth and accrual rates at different ages of retirement

| Last Year of Work | Italy | | France | | Netherlands | | Spain | |
|---|---|---|---|---|---|---|---|---|
| | SSW[a] | ACCR | SSW[b] | ACCR | SSW[c] | ACCR | SSW[d] | ACCR |
| 54 | 285,353 | 0 | 792,068 | 0 | 266,958 | 0 | 11,343.7 | 0 |
| 55 | 280,477 | −0.017 | 886,083 | 0.12 | 247,365 | −0.073 | 11,006.9 | −0.030 |
| 56 | 274,486 | −0.021 | 986,531 | 0.11 | 229,033 | −0.074 | 10,836.9 | −0.015 |
| 57 | 268,066 | −0.023 | 1,034,081 | 0.05 | 212,121 | −0.074 | 10,598.0 | −0.022 |
| 58 | 261,160 | −0.026 | 1,029,771 | 0.00 | 196,668 | −0.073 | 10,025.0 | −0.054 |
| 59 | 253,918 | −0.028 | 1,024,586 | −0.01 | 296,367 | 0.507 | 9,566.8 | −0.046 |
| 60 | 241,677 | −0.048 | 954,881 | −0.07 | 258,463 | −0.128 | 9,809.7 | 0.025 |
| 61 | 229,536 | −0.050 | 892,339 | −0.07 | 222,715 | −0.138 | 10,008.0 | 0.020 |
| 62 | 217,643 | −0.052 | 826,880 | −0.07 | 188,559 | −0.153 | 10,193.3 | 0.019 |
| 63 | 205,963 | −0.054 | 768,327 | −0.07 | 157,316 | −0.166 | 10,117.1 | −0.007 |
| 64 | 194,396 | −0.056 | 710,313 | −0.08 | 128,554 | −0.183 | 9,860.6 | −0.025 |
| 65 | 183,099 | −0.058 | 656,799 | −0.08 | 120,371 | −0.064 | 8,629.4 | −0.125 |
| 66 | 172,011 | −0.061 | 607,337 | −0.08 | 112,631 | −0.064 | 7,364.4 | −0.147 |
| 67 | 161,167 | −0.063 | 559,482 | −0.08 | 105,331 | −0.065 | 6,067.9 | −0.176 |
| 68 | 150,577 | −0.066 | 513,035 | −0.08 | 98,468 | −0.065 | 4,815.7 | −0.206 |
| 69 | 140,269 | −0.068 | 468,382 | −0.09 | 92,038 | −0.065 | 3,608.2 | −0.251 |

*Source:* Gruber and Wise (1999a).
*Note:* The table presents the base-case incentive calculations. The simulations consider typically a married man who was born in 1930 and who planned to retire early in 1985. For a closer description of the simulation model for each country, see Gruber and Wise (1999a).
a. In 1,000 lira.
b. In French francs.
c. In guilder.
d. In 1,000 peseta.

accruals would induce the worker to retire at age 55. If he or she were more forward looking and measured the value of immediate retirement versus the value at the optimal date when social security wealth is maximized, then he would continue to work until age 60. In this example, the predictions of retirement behavior differ according to the approaches followed. However, in countries like Spain that have a similar pattern of accrual rates, future gains in social security wealth never compensate for the initial losses. Thus, the worker receives maximal social security wealth when retiring at age 55. The same result holds for the United States.[3]

## 3.3   Option-Value Approach

A third approach for measuring incentives for retirement was introduced by Stock and Wise (1990a, 1990b). This forward-looking measure considers the entire future path of accruals to social security
wealth and the future stream of wage income due to continued work.
If a worker retires early, then he may maximize social security wealth
but forgoes further wage income. Consider a worker at age $A$ who considers retiring at age $R$ and compares the discounted value of retiring
at age $R$ to the discounted value of retiring at age $R^o$, at which time the
sum of wage income and social security wealth is maximized. The difference defines the option value, which gets lost if the worker retires at
an age different from $R^o$. The option value of continued work can be
written as

$$OV_A(R^o) = \sum_{t=R}^{R^o-1} LABIN_t^{NET} \cdot (1+r)^{-(t-A)} + SSW_A(R^o) - SSW_A(R),$$

where $LABIN_t^{NET}$ denotes the net labor income at age $t$. The option
value defines the loss of retiring at age $R \neq R^o$. The assumption is that
the person will continue to work if this option value is positive. Note
that $R^o$ may be different from retirement age $R^*$, when social security
wealth is maximized. Social security wealth is lost before reaching retirement age $R^*$. Therefore, the continuation of working before age $R^*$
always increases the discounted value of postponing retirement since
labor income adds simply to social security wealth gains. However,
the decision to retire after age $R^*$ may lead to an increase in the discounted sum of future wage incomes and future accruals of social
security wealth. If additional labor income exceeds the loss of social
security wealth when retiring after age $R^*$, then the discounted value
of retiring later than $R^*$ increases. Hence, the worker will continue to
work until age $R^o > R^*$. The option-value approach comprises the
entire future streams of income and wealth accruals. Both components
of continued work are taken into account—the wage earnings and the
change in future social security accruals.

In a more general version, the option-value approach is able to take
into account nonfinancial retirement incentives as well. It involves the
maximization of a utility function that depends not only on income
but also on leisure. In this way, the option value captures substitution
effects and also an income effect: if social security wealth increases, the

individual increases consumption of normal goods, and to the extent that leisure is a normal good, he retires earlier. The reason for the advantage of this approach (to take into account nonfinancial incentives like leisure by using a utility function) is also the reason for its flaw: one has to determine a particular utility function, which may not capture appropriately the individuals' preferences. In many studies, option values suggest an optimal retirement age after age 70, which is inconsistent with observed retirement ages between age 55 and 65. This may indicate that the preferences underlying the option-value model are not consistent with individual-choice behavior. Another disadvantage is that the option value depends crucially on the individual's wage—both because the wage enters directly into the calculation of the option value and because it serves as a basis for calculation of social security wealth. Therefore, a lot of the variation of the option value comes from the variation in wages. Wages could, however, be correlated with underlying taste for work if, for example, the high-wage earners are in favor of continuing work. If this correlation is not taken into account, then estimates of the effects of changes in retirement incentives on retirement might be biased.

Compared to peak value, option value does not focus solely on financial incentives. Hence, the disadvantage of option value is that it does not, unlike peak value, isolate a source of variation of retirement that is less subject to biases from omitted unobserved characteristics. The advantage of option value is that it can explain a lot of variation that peak value leaves unexplained.

## 3.4   Empirical Evidence for Retirement Incentives

The crucial question for social security systems—how program incentives affect retirement behavior—has been examined in a large number of empirical studies. In this section, we give a brief survey of the latest studies of this kind.[4]

Coile and Gruber (2000a) use data available through the University of Michigan Health and Retirement Survey (HRS) (supported by the National Institute on Aging) to investigate the impact of U.S. social security incentives on male retirement. In a regression, they analyze potential determinants of retirement, such as social security wealth, age dummies, earnings, and a specification for the incentive variable (accrual, peak value, or option value). They find that forward-looking measures that take account of the entire future stream of social security wealth accruals have a much larger impact on retirement decisions than incentives measures based on the accrual over the next year. Hence, forward-looking measures like the peak value are important variables for estimating the financial incentives for retirement. Furthermore, they control for a health variable (the self-reported health status) and a variable indicating health insurance coverage. However, these variables are difficult to interpret directly. Instead, the authors include these measures to ensure that their omission does not significantly bias the retirement incentive estimates. The result is that those variables do not change the estimates of the other variables.

Mitchell and Phillips (2000) extend the economic opportunities available to older workers by including disability benefits. A reduction of early retirement benefits may induce some workers to stay on the job to the normal retirement age, while perhaps prompting others to seek social security disability insurance benefits. They observe the retirement path that was chosen by individuals in the Health and Retirement Survey—disability retirement prior to age 65, early retirement between 62 and 64, and normal retirement at 65. The authors model the choice of retirement options as a function of the expected present value of the wealth and leisure that are associated with each pathway. They find that individuals with higher wealth tend to retire earlier. In a second estimation, an interaction term between leisure and poor health is added where health is measured by a self-reported health status. The effect of leisure is positive but statistically insignificant. The effect of health is that people reporting to be in poor health value leisure differently than do those in better health, but the estimated effect is statistically insignificant. The simulation of a cut in early retirement benefits results in fewer people choosing early retirement as their preferred path but more people opting for disability pensions.

Blundell, Meghir, and Smith (2002) evaluate the economic incentives for retirement underlying the United Kingdom's pension system. They use a sample of men age 55 or older from the UK Retirement Survey. Total pension wealth and accrual measures are built up from combining the basic state pension, the state earnings-related scheme, occupational pensions, and disability benefits. As incentive measures, they employ the one-period accrual or the option value. The results show that pension wealth and incentive variables are jointly significant. As expected, the wealth effect is positive, and the accrual effect is negative. The negative coefficient of the option value indicates that the greater the forgone future opportunities from stopping working now, the less

likely individuals are to retire. However, they find that disability benefits alone appear to have little impact on retirement decisions.

In a recent multicountry project, Gruber and Wise (2002) estimate
the effect of retirement incentives on the individual level on retirement
behavior using microdata for workers observed at different ages. In
each of the 12 country studies, experts estimate the probability of retirement, based on the incentives of the countries' social security systems. In a first step, they compute social security wealth (SSW) for
every pathway to retirement (normal retirement, disability, unemployment, and early retirement). Then they calculate a weighted SSW in
which the weights correspond to the weights of the different retirement
paths for the worker with the median wage at different retirement
ages. In a second step, the retirement incentives that are inherent in
the social security systems are measured by the single-year accruals of
SSW, the peak value, and the option value for the median values as
well as the 10th and 90th percentile values. In a third step, they estimate a probit model with retirement as a dependent variable and various combinations of independent variables—sex, average lifetime,
education, industry of employment, earnings, social security wealth, a
specification for the incentive variable (accrual, peak value, or option
value), and a specification for the age variable (linear or dummy
variable).

Concerning social security wealth, it is assumed that persons with
greater wealth are more likely to retire early. Individual differences in
wage earnings are used as a proxy for differences in the preference for
work versus retirement so that the variable wage earnings is intended
to control for this kind of heterogeneity among individuals. The prediction with respect to age is that persons are more likely to prefer retirement to work as they get older. The linear age variable is intended
to capture the age effect but only if preferences for leisure evolve lin-
early with age. If this is not the case, an age indicator variable is able
to control for these nonlinearities. So the retirement rate at certain ages
is larger than at other ages. For example, in the United States, the retirement rate at age 65 is higher, which may be caused by customary
retirement behavior. Since age 65 is the normal retirement age, many
employees may think that 65 is *the* age to retire. Furthermore, employees typically retire after the age at which persons are first eligible for benefits. The retirement rate after that age is significantly larger
than would be predicted on the basis of financial measures alone. The
reason seems to be that few employees have saved enough to retire

without relying exclusively on public- or employer-provided pension benefits. The indicator variables for each age control for these effects.

The striking result in virtually all countries is that the retirement incentives of social security programs are strongly related to early retirement. In seven countries—Belgium, Canada, Denmark, France, Germany, Japan, and Sweden—almost all estimated effects of the three incentive measures and under both age specifications are negatively related to retirement age and significantly different from zero. In Italy and Spain, the peak-value and the option-value effects are typically not significant and sometimes have the wrong sign. In two countries, the Netherlands and the United States, the effect of the single-year accrual measure is positive, while estimations based on the other incentive measures show the expected negative sign and are significant. The estimations for the United Kingdom show the predicted negative effects but are sometimes insignificant. All in all, the results from the 12 country analyses confirm the conjecture that social security systems matter greatly in early retirement decisions. The incentives inherent in retirement programs are clear determinants of individual retirement behavior. The results reveal a strong relationship between incentive effects and labor-force participation of older persons, independent of economic, social, and cultural differences among countries.

# 4 Optimal Design and Reform

## 4.1 Introduction

Chapters 4, 5, 6, and 7 are exclusively theoretical. At the center of the analysis is a worker with a given productivity and utility function who tries to maximize his or her lifetime welfare by optimally choosing a consumption vector and a labor supply. Ideally, labor supply is time-dependent and decreases progressively until the end of life as both productivity and health decline, but here we divide a lifetime into two periods: individuals work the whole first period and just a part of the second period (until retirement). We also let the worker choose a different intensity of labor in each of the two periods. In some examples, the labor supply is fixed, and only the age of retirement varies. In other examples, we study only one period. As far as policy tools are concerned, we consider only linear instruments (except in chapter 7). We realize that nonlinear taxes and transfers are welfare superior, and we refer to work that uses them.

These restrictions reflect real-life constraints. We live in a world with mandatory retirement ages and discrete length of week-work hours where tax schedules and benefit structures cannot take any shape.

In this chapter, we lay down the basic model of retirement choice that is used in this book. We focus on labor distortions and how they depend on the type of social security chosen—pay as you go (PAYG) or fully funded (FF), contributory or redistributive, defined benefits or defined contributions. We abstract from other aspects that have been developed in previous work, and our major references are the OECD countries (especially the continental European countries). If the rate of activity among elderly workers varies greatly in countries with a predominant PAYG first pillar and a similar standard of living, we believe it is because of the incentive structure of their social security schemes.

Fabel (1994) distinguishes three theoretical approaches to retirement behavior. The first one focuses on disability retirement rules. This approach—adopted notably by Diamond and Mirrlees (1978, 1986)—considers disability as contingent and moral hazard as influencing the design of social security benefits. We discuss it in chapter 7. The second approach is concerned with labor contracts and retirement clauses. Lazear (1979) is an example of this approach. Accordingly, social security and private pension arrangements are viewed as discipline devices that preclude shirking on the job. This is discussed in chapter 8. Finally, there is the induced-retirement approach, which relates the retirement decision to the income opportunities provided by public and also private pension plans. Feldstein (1974) was one of the first to study induced retirement within a two-period model where the retirement decision is identified with second-period labor supply.[1] Chapters 4 and 5 follow this approach, particularly the one developed by Crawford and Lilien (1981), who discuss how departing from assumptions of perfect capital markets, actuarial fairness, and certain lifetimes affects retirement.

In this book, we assume that individuals are perfectly rational and that government respects their preferences when designing optimal retirement policies. In fact, one of the rationales for social security is the individual's myopia: some individuals consume all of their earnings before retirement and yet would be happy if someone (here, the state) would force them to save for retirement. In a recent paper, Diamond and Köszegi (2003) show that when retirement is endogenous, there are two sources of inefficient and unprepared retirement—traditional undersaving and early retirement. They follow Laibson's (1997) approach, which distinguishes between earlier selves and later selves. Earlier selves are tempted to save too little and to retire too early, relative to what their later selves would do, and the interaction between these two decisions can paradoxically lead to too much saving. Diamond and Köszegi also show how traditional social security policies that fulfill the preferences of the later selves are to be modified. This is clearly an interesting approach but still too underdeveloped to be presented here.

## 4.2   The Basic Model

In the canonical model of overlapping generations that we use, people live for three periods of equal length (25 years). The first period is one of full dependence: individuals live with their parents, and we are not really concerned with it. Then comes the period of full activity, which we use to denote the generation to which they belong. Members of generation $t$ consume $c_t$ in period $t$ and supply an amount of labor $l_t$. In the third period, $t + 1$, they consume $d_{t+1}$ and work a fraction $z_{t+1}$ of that period with a labor supply $h_{t+1}$.

If the length of each period is 25 years, this implies that a member of generation $t$ starts his life at $t - 1$. He becomes autonomous at time $t$; he works a fraction $l_t$ of these 25 years. In period $t + 1$, he works for $z_{t+1} \times 25$ years, and during that period of activity he supplies an amount of labor equal to $h_{t+1}z_{t+1}25$. His length of retirement is thus $(1 - z_{t+1})25$ years.

In what follows, we normalize each period to 1, ignore the period of dependence, and call $z$ the age of retirement—even though formally the age of retirement is $2 + z$. Individuals get utility from consumption $c$ and $d$, from leisure $1 - l$ and $1 - h$, and from retirement $1 - z$.

For the time being, we assume a small open economy[2] with a given wage rate $w$ and an interest rate $r = R - 1$. Population grows at a constant rate $n$. Individual preferences are represented by a utility function with standard properties:

$$u_t = u(c_t, l_t) + \beta u(d_{t+1}, h_{t+1}, z_{t+1}), \tag{4.1}$$

where $\beta$ is a factor of time preference. In a pure laissez-faire economy, the problem of any member of generation $t$ is

$$Max_{l,h,z} \, u(wl_t - s_t, l_t) + \beta u(wh_{t+1}z_{t+1} + Rs_t, h_{t+1}, z_{t+1}),$$

where $s$ denotes saving. For reasons of convenience, we posit that $s$ can take any value, thus assuming away liquidity constraints. The first-order conditions (FOCs) for an interior maximum are

$$\left. \begin{array}{ll} u_{c_t} = \beta u_{d_{t+1}}R; & u_{c_t}w = -u_{l_t}; \\ u_{d_{t+1}}wz_{t+1} = -u_{h_{t+1}}; & u_{d_{t+1}}wh_{t+1} = -u_{z_{t+1}} \end{array} \right\}, \tag{4.2}$$

where the subscripts denote partial derivatives ($u_c = \partial u(c, l)/\partial c$).

Up to now, we have implicitly assumed that individuals are identical within the generation to which they belong. Suppose now that they differ in labor productivity. In other words, we now have $w^i$ with $i = 1, \ldots, I$ and frequency $\pi^i$. We use superscript $i$ to denote type $i$'s individuals. For the sake of simplicity, we use the operator $E$ for $\sum \pi^i$.

## 4.3 Pension Systems

We now introduce a public pension system that is characterized by two features—(1) whether it is fully funded (FF) or based on the pay-as-you-go (PAYG) principle and (2) whether it is contributory (Bismarckian) or redistributive (Beveridgean).

Let us denote the overall pension benefit of individuals $i$ by $P^i$. With a PAYG system, we have

$$\tau E(wl_t(1+n) + wh_t z_t) = EP_t,$$

where $\tau$ is the payroll-tax-rate constant over time and across periods.[3] Note that with a FF system, we have

$$\tau E(wl_t R + wh_{t+1} z_{t+1}) = EP_{t+1}.$$

Throughout this chapter, we assume that $R \geq 1 + n$, which seems to be the reasonable hypothesis.

Our concern is the effect of the pension system on retirement decisions. We use the concept of net social security wealth—namely, the present value of benefits minus contributions. We denote this net social security wealth as $\Theta_t$. We are also interested in $\theta_{t+1} = -\partial \Theta_t / \partial z_{t+1} R$, which is the marginal effect of $z_t$ on social security wealth. Here, $\Theta_t$ is a measure of the average actuarial fairness of the system, and $\theta_t$ measures the marginal fairness of the system. In terms of effect on retirement decisions, $\Theta_t$ acts as an income effect, and $\theta_t$ acts as a substitution effect. In the literature, $\theta_t$ is called the *tax distortion* and also the *implicit tax on postponed activity*.

We now introduce the parameters of the pension system in the lifetime budget constant of an individual:

$$c_t^i + d_{t+1}^i / R = w^i (1 - \tau)(l_t^i + h_{t+1}^i z_{t+1}^i / R) + P_{t+1}^i / R$$

or

$$c_t^i + d_{t+1}^i / R = w^i (l_t^i + h_{t+1}^i z_{t+1}^i / R) + \Theta_t^i.$$

Substituting this constraint in the utility function (4.1) and maximizing with respect to $z_{t+1}^i$, we get

$$u_{d_{t+1}}^i (h_{t+1}^i w^i - \theta_{t+1}^i) = -u_{z_{t+1}}^i.$$

Clearly, $\theta_{t+1}^i$ introduces a wedge between the marginal productivity and the marginal disutility of working one more year.

To get an explicit expression for $\Theta_t$, we have to specify another feature of the pension system: is it contributory, or is it redistributive? The extreme case of a redistributive system is one that provides a flat-rate pension while being financed by a payroll tax that is proportional to earned income. Such a system is sometimes called *Beveridgean*. In a purely contributory system (called *Bismarckian*), retirees get a pension that is related to their contributions. With a fully funded system, there is equality between the present values of benefits and contributions. With a pay-as-you-go system, there is a difference between the two that depends on the gap between $R$ and $1 + n$, the rate of return on the capital market, and the rate of return of contributions to a PAYG scheme.

We consider a mixed PAYG system with a fraction $\alpha$ of Bismarck and $(1 - \alpha)$ of Beveridge. Accordingly,

$$\Theta_t^i = -\tau\{w^i l_t^i (1 - \alpha(1 + n)/R) - (1 - \alpha)Ewl_{t+1}(1 + n)/R$$

$$+ (1 - \alpha)w^i h_{t+1}^i z_{t+1}^i/R - (1 - \alpha)Ewh_{t+1}z_{t+1}/R\}.$$

On this basis, we now assess the fairness, average and marginal, of alternative systems.

1. FF (or PAYG with $R = 1 + n$) with $\alpha = 1$:

$$\Theta_t^i = 0 \quad \text{and} \quad \theta_{t+1}^i = 0.$$

This is not surprising. A purely contributory PAYG system is equivalent to a purely contributory FF system when the rates of return of the two are identical. They are neutral both on average and at the margin. Note, however, that this holds only when there is no liquidity-constraints problem. When $\tau$ is high enough and there are liquidity constraints, individuals would like to unsave to neutralize what can be viewed as excessive forced saving. This caveat shows that there is a difference between an individualized but mandatory fully funded pension system and conventional private saving.[4]

2. PAYG with $R > 1 + n$ and $\alpha = 1$:

$$\Theta_t^i = -\tau w^i l_t^i \left(1 - \frac{1 + n}{R}\right) < 0 \quad \text{and} \quad \theta_{t+1}^i = 0.$$

A Bismarckian PAYG system generates a negative social security wealth, something that is well known. This is equivalent to a negative income effect, and if retirement is a normal good, it should increase the age of retirement.

3. FF (or PAYG with $R = 1 + n$) and $\alpha = 0$:

$$\Theta_t^i = -\tau\{w^i l_t^i - E w l_t + (w^i h_{t+1}^i z_{t+1}^i - E w h_{t+1} z_{t+1})/R\}$$

$$\text{and} \quad \theta_{t+1}^i = \tau w^i h_{t+1}^i.$$

Quite clearly, individuals earning less than average will have positive social security wealth, and those with earned income above mean income will have negative social security wealth. Again, with retirement being a normal good, this will yield income effects going in opposite directions. Such a system distorts retirement choice: marginally, it is not actuarially fair. Hence, for low-income retirees, the two effects go in the same direction—namely, earlier retirement. For high-income retirees, there is some ambiguity.

4. PAYG with $R > 1 + n$ and $\alpha = 0$:

$$\Theta_t^i = -\tau\left\{ w^i l_t^i - \frac{1+n}{R} E w l_t + (w^i h_{t+1}^i z_{t+1}^i - E w h_{t+1} z_{t+1})/R \right\}$$

$$\text{and} \quad \theta_{t+1}^i = \tau w^i h_{t+1}^i. \tag{4.3}$$

When the rate of interest is higher than the rate of population growth, social security wealth decreases even more. However, the implicit tax is not modified.

## 4.4  A Double Burden

In the above presentation, we use the concept of total pension $P_{t+1}^i$—namely, the sum of yearly benefits. If, instead, we use the concept of yearly benefit $p_{t+1}^i$, such that

$$P_{t+1}^i = (1 - z_{t+1}^i)p_{t+1}^i,$$

nothing would change for contributory systems. However, things would change with a Beveridgean system. Instead of considering a uniform value for $\bar{P}$, we now consider a uniform value for $\bar{p}$. In that case, social security wealth can be expressed as

$$\Theta_t^i = -\tau w^i l_t^i - \tau w^i h_{t+1}^i z_{t+1}^i/R + (1 - z_{t+1}^i)\bar{p}_{t+1}/R,$$

where

$$\bar{p}_t(1 - \bar{z}_t) = \tau[Ewl_t(1 + n) + Ewh_t z_t].$$

We thus write

$$\Theta_t^i = -\tau \left\{ w^i l_t^i - \frac{1 - z_{t+1}^i}{1 - \bar{z}_{t+1}} \frac{1 + n}{R} Ewl_{t+1} \right.$$

$$\left. + \left( w^i h_{t+1}^i z_{t+1}^i - \frac{1 - z_{t+1}^i}{1 - \bar{z}_{t+1}} Ewh_{t+1} z_{t+1} \right) \middle/ R \right\}$$

and

$$\theta_{t+1}^i = w^i h_{t+1}^i \left( \tau + \frac{\bar{p}_{t+1}}{w^i h_{t+1}^i} \right). \tag{4.4}$$

It is interesting to compare (4.3) and (4.4). According to (4.3), one more year of work implies an annual tax of $\tau w^i h_t^i$. According to (4.4), it implies not only such a tax but also the forgone benefit of $\bar{p}_{t+1}$. Which of these alternative systems is the most relevant is an empirical question. As shown by Gruber and Wise (1999a), a number of countries have a tax on postponed activity that includes both burdens—the payroll tax itself and the forgone benefits. In some other countries, the total amount of pensions received is independent of the age of retirement.[5]

Note that in a mixed regime the implicit tax is given by

$$\theta_{t+1}^i = (1 - \alpha)(\tau w^i h_{t+1}^i + \bar{p}_{t+1}).$$

In table 4.1, we present these different implicit-tax cases.

Widely used individualized notional accounts[6] can be defined as being PAYG and Bismarckian. Because they are mandatory, they generate distortion even when $R = 1 + n$ for those subject to liquidity constraints.

**Table 4.1**
Implicit tax on postponed retirement

|  | Uniform Aggregate Benefit | Uniform Yearly Benefit |
| --- | --- | --- |
| $\alpha = 1$ | 0 | 0 |
| $0 < \alpha < 1$ | $\tau w^i h_{t+1}^i (1 - \alpha)$ | $w^i h_t^i \left( \tau + \frac{\bar{p}}{w^i h^i} \right)(1 - \alpha)$ |
| $\alpha = 0$ | $\tau w^i h_{t+1}^i$ | $w^i h_t^i \left( \tau + \frac{\bar{p}}{w^i h^i} \right)$ |

Most public pension schemes are either *defined-benefit* (DB) plans or *defined-contributions* (DC) plans. In defined-benefit plans, $p_t^i = \bar{\varrho}w_{t-1}^i$ — namely, pension are equal to a fraction (replacement ratio $\bar{\varrho}$) of previous earnings. In defined-contribution plans, $p_t^i = \hat{\varrho}\tau w_{t-1}^i$, where $\hat{\varrho}$ is the rate of return of the system—$1 + n$ if PAYG or $R$ if FF. In the current abstract setting without uncertainty, the two rules are equivalent. In general, however, a defined-contribution system tends to be more neutral toward the retirement decision than a defined-benefit system is. Defined-benefit schemes, private or public, include restrictions such as minimal career years, mandatory retirement age, and earnings tests.

## 4.5 Optimal Tax Rates

Up to now, we have assumed given and unique payroll taxes. Both taxes and benefits affect labor supply, retirement, income distribution, and social welfare (at least when $\alpha < 1$). It can thus be interesting to try to derive the optimal levels of payroll taxes, allowing for different values in the two periods. To simplify matters, we make a number of additional assumptions. First, we assume that $\alpha = 0$ and that aggregate pension benefits are uniform. Second, we adopt a quasi-linear utility function to eliminate income effects. Third, we assume that $R = 1 + n$ and thus neglect any intergenerational redistribution. This allows us to focus on the steady state. As a fourth assumption, we consider a social planner with a utilitarian objective. Finally, we keep our assumption of no liquidity constraints. With these assumptions, we want to calculate the optimal payroll tax rates.

We thus use an individual utility function, such as

$$u^i = u(c^i - v(l^i)) + \beta u(d^i - v(h^i)\varphi(z_{t+1})),$$

where $v(\cdot)$ and $\varphi(\cdot)$ are convex functions further constrained to keep the problem convex. The problem of the social planner can be expressed by the following Lagrangian function:

$$\mathcal{L} = E[u(wl^*(1 - \tau_1) - s^* - v(l^*)) + \beta u(wh^*z^*(1 - \tau_2) + Rs^*$$
$$+ P - v(h^*)\varphi(z^*))] - \mu[P - \tau_1(1 + n)Ewl - \tau_2 Ewhz],$$

where $\mu$ is the Lagrange multiplier associated with the revenue constraint, and $\tau_1$ and $\tau_2$ are the two payroll taxes to be determined. We assume that $s$, $l$, $h$, and $z$ have been optimally chosen and use the envelope theorem.

The first-order conditions for an interior optimum are

$$\frac{\partial \mathscr{L}}{\partial \tau_1} = -Eu_c wl + \mu(1+n)\left[Ewl + E\tau_1 w \frac{\partial l}{\partial \tau_1}\right] = 0$$

$$\frac{\partial \mathscr{L}}{\partial \tau_2} = -\beta Eu_d whz + \mu\left[Ewhz + E\tau_2 w\left(h\frac{\partial z}{\partial \tau_2} + z\frac{\partial h}{\partial \tau_2}\right)\right] = 0$$

$$\frac{\partial \mathscr{L}}{\partial P} = \beta Eu_d - \mu = 0.$$

After some simplifications, we obtain the following tax formulas:

$$\tau_1 = \frac{cov(u_c, wl)}{Eu_d Ew \dfrac{\partial l}{\partial \tau_1}},$$

and

$$\tau_2 = \frac{cov(u_d, whz)}{Eu_d Ew\left(h\dfrac{\partial z}{\partial \tau_2} + z\dfrac{\partial h}{\partial \tau_2}\right)},$$

where $cov(u_c, wl)$ and $cov(u_d, whz)$ reflect a concern for equity and are known to be negative.[7] In the denominator, we have $\partial l/\partial \tau_1$, $\partial z/\partial \tau_2$, and $\partial h/\partial \tau_2$ (all negative), which give the effect of payroll taxation on either labor supply or the age of retirement.[8] These denominators represent the efficiency terms. A high elasticity implies that the tax is costly on efficiency grounds and should be low.

One can conjecture that $\tau_2 < \tau_1$ for two reasons. First, unlike $\tau_1$, $\tau_2$ has two disincentive effects—one on $h$ and one on $z$. Second, $z$, the retirement age, seems more sensitive to taxation than the "weekly" labor supply $l$ or $h$.

## 4.6 Retirement and Social Security Reform

It is often implied that moving from a pay-as-you-go pension system to a fully funded one will have a number of beneficial effects, including that of inducing workers to retire later. This belief rests on the idea that within a fully funded system distortions tend to be smaller than within a pay-as-you-go system. Is this really the case? To answer this question as clearly as possible, we distinguish between two types of reforms. The first one consists of moving toward a fully funded system, while keeping both inter- and intragenerational redistributions unchanged. The second reform implies shifting toward a FF system, preserving the entitlements of the transitional generation through some kind of grandfathering, and introducing individualized pension rights for future generations.

Consider the first reform. We start from a pay-as-you-go system with a flat-rate benefit and optimal linear payroll taxes $\tau_1$ and $\tau_2$. We use the simple overlapping-generations model with inelastic labor supply and quadratic utility for retirement:

$$u^i = u(w^i(1 - \tau_1) - s^i) + \beta u(w^i(1 - \tau_2)z^i + Rs^i + P - (z^i)^2/2\gamma),$$

where $\gamma$ is a health parameter. Within such a setting, each generation has to pay to service the implicit debt associated with the presence of a PAYG system: $\tau\overline{w}(R - (1 - n))$. The social security reform makes the debt explicit, but the payment remains to be made each period. After the reform, we have a budget constraint

$$\tau_1\overline{w}R + \tau_2 Ewz = P + \tau_1\overline{w}(R - (1 + n)).$$

The left side of the equation is total revenue, and the right side consists of pension benefits and the service of a now explicit debt. This constraint is identical to the one with the PAYG system:

$$\tau_1\overline{w}(1 + n) + \tau_2 Ewz = P.$$

We keep the same tax rates $\tau_1$ and $\tau_2$ because we want to implement the same intragenerational redistribution as before. As these tax rates were determined optimally, there is no way to have a welfare-improving tax reform. As a consequence, the age of retirement remains unchanged:

$$z^i = \gamma w^i(1 - \tau_2).$$

Now consider the second reform. The transition generation is compensated for the shift, but from there on pension benefits become generated by a fully funded partially individualized system. The service of the debt is to be financed by a flat tax in the first period ($\theta$). We now have

$$P^i = (\tau_1 - \theta)\overline{w}R + \tau_2 w^i z^i$$

and

$$u^i = u(w^i(1 - \tau_1) - s^i) + \beta u(w^i z^i + Rs^i + (\tau_1 - \theta)\overline{w}R - (z^i)^2/2\gamma).$$

Now the retirement age has clearly increased for all elderly workers:

$$z^i = \gamma w^i.$$

It is possible that by removing such a distortion on the retirement age, individuals can be made better off.[9] This does not come from the shift to a FF system but from the removal of the distortion. In other words, keeping the PAYG scheme and removing the distortion could make everyone better off.[10]

## 4.7   Earnings Tests and Retirement

In a number of countries, social security systems have earnings tests: an individual whose earnings exceed a certain ceiling faces a reduction in social security benefits. Some countries do not have this test. Others have them but in variable forms. In the United States, means tests have been suppressed, but for a long time they applied to retirees age 65 to 70. The earnings test does not apply to capital and rental incomes or to other pensions. The ceiling and the percentage of reduction also vary from country to country. Table 4.2 presents the earnings tests found in a sample of countries.

Why do we have earning tests? Are they socially desirable? Before answering these two questions, we note that earning tests are rarely questioned in the case of unemployment insurance. Also, in a number

**Table 4.2**
Earnings tests, various countries

|  | Ceiling (percentage of average earning) | Reduction Rate (percentage) |
| --- | --- | --- |
| Canada | 160 | 15 |
| Greece | 116 | 100 |
| Denmark | 50 | 60 |
| Austria | 30 | 100 |
| Belgium | 33 | 100 |
| Norway | 18 | 50 |
| Australia | 8 | 50 |
| Ireland | None | 100 |
| Portugal | None | 100 |
| Spain | None | 100 |

*Source:* Disney and Smith (2002).

of welfare programs, benefits are subject to means testing of both earnings and all other sources of income.[11]

There are three rationales for earnings tests in social security. The
first one is redistributive: in a second-best world, it may be desirable
to tax earnings after the statutory age of retirement at a higher rate
than other sources of income including pension benefits. We return to
this rationale later.

The second argument is related to the idea that forcing elderly
workers into retirement fosters employment of the young. As we show
in chapter 8, which examines the demand side, this belief is as widespread as it is ill-founded.

The third argument applies to heavily redistributive pension systems and is behind means testing for welfare benefits: benefit are
granted because people are without any other resources; if they are
shown to have resources, they are not entitled to assistance. This argument should not be used for contributory pension systems.

Clearly, only the first argument could apply to the majority of social
security systems. But as we show below, it could apply as well to
the issue of subsidizing earnings after retirement. Before looking at
that, let us mention the existing evidence (Friedberg, 2000; Disney and
Smith, 2002), which suggests that the abolition of the earnings tests
where they existed had a small but significant impact on labor supply.

To discuss the desirability of earnings tests, we use an economy in
which individuals live for one period divided into three parts—work
before formal retirement at age $\bar{z}$, work after formal retirement until
age $z^i$, and retirement of length $1 - z^i$. Individuals are distinguished
only according to their wage.

The problem is to maximize the sum of individual utilities subject to
the revenue constraint:

$$\sum \pi^i (\tau w^i l^i \bar{z} + \tau_a w_a^i l_a^i (z^i - \bar{z})) = E(\tau w l z + \tau_a w_a l_a (z - \bar{z})) = (1 - \bar{z})p,$$

where $\bar{z}$ is the legal age of retirement, $z^i$ the age of definitive retirement, $w^i$ the wage before $\bar{z}$, $w_a^i$ the wage after $\bar{z}$, $l^i$ the labor supply before $\bar{z}$, $l_a^i$ the labor supply after $\bar{z}$, $\tau$ and $\tau_a$ the tax rate before and after
formal retirement, and $p$ the flat-rate pension.

We now turn to the central question: are earnings tests socially desirable? We use the above model with two modifications: there is now
a statutory age of retirement at which individuals start drawing pen-

sion benefits and after which individuals can continue working at a different pace and different wage. What we want to represent is the idea that after the legal age of retirement some individuals can work but for fewer hours and at a lower productivity than before this age. They will do that for some time $(z^i - \bar{z})$ and then retire definitively. The individual of type $i$ (that is, with productivity $w^i$ and $w_a^i$) has a utility

$$u^i = u(c^i, l^i, l_a^i, z^i, \bar{z}) = u(c^i) - v(l^i)\varphi(\bar{z}) - v(l_a^i)(\varphi(z^i) - \varphi(\bar{z}))$$

and a budget constraint

$$c^i = w^i l^i \bar{z}(1 - \tau) + w_a^i l_a^i (z^i - \bar{z})(1 - \tau_a) + p(1 - \bar{z}).$$

This simple model takes into account the idea that at age $\bar{z}$ workers have an increasing disutility for labor. This means that for the same net wages they will work fewer hours after than before the legal age of retirement $\bar{z}$. Furthermore, employment after formal retirement is different than preretirement employment. One can thus expect that $w_a^i < w^i$ for all and that the decline will be more important for certain types of occupation (such as those requesting physical strength) than for others (such as those requesting experience).

We are interested in comparing $\tau$ and $\tau_a$. If $\tau_a > \tau$, earnings after formal retirement are more heavily taxed than before formal retirement. The problem for the social planner is expressed by the following Lagrangian function:

$$\mathscr{L} = E[u(c, l, l_a, z, \bar{z}) - \mu((1 - \bar{z})p - \tau w l z - \tau_a w_a l_a (z - \bar{z}))].$$

In Lozachmeur et al. (2004), we derive the following formulas for $\tau$ and $\tau_a$:

$$\tau = \frac{cov(u'(c), \bar{z}wl)}{\dfrac{\mu}{1 - \bar{z}} Ew\bar{z} \dfrac{\partial \tilde{l}}{\partial \tau_a}}$$

$$\tau_a = \frac{cov(u'(c), w_a l_a(z - \bar{z}))}{\dfrac{\mu}{1 - \bar{z}} \left[ Ew_a(z - \bar{z}) \dfrac{\partial \tilde{l}_a}{\partial \tau_a} + Ew_a l_a \dfrac{\partial \tilde{z}}{\partial \tau_a} \right]},$$

where $\mu$ is the cost of public funds. Those tax rates depend on two terms—(1) an efficiency term (the denominator), which gives the compensated effect of the tax on the weekly labor supply for $\tau$ and on both the weekly labor supply and the age of retirement for $\tau_a$, and (2) an equity term (the numerator), which is the (negative) covariance between marginal utility and gross earnings.

Not surprisingly, the desirability of earning tests is an empirical question. To illustrate this point, we take two extreme examples. First, assume that after age $\bar{z}$ all wages decrease and converge on a unique value. There is not much ground for a redistributive tax after formal retirement, and thus $\tau_a < \tau$. Then assume that the wage dispersion increases after formal retirement. Those with low productivity see their productivity fall to zero, and those with high productivity keep high levels of wage income. In that extreme case, an earnings test is clearly desirable.

In these two extreme cases, we have focused on the equity terms. Turning to the efficiency term, it is clear that if both $l_a$ and $z$ are more elastic than $l$, then $\tau$ is likely to be higher than $\tau_a$, all things being equal. In Cremer, Lozachmeur, and Pestieau (2004b), the same question is dealt with in a nonlinear tax setting. Roughly speaking, the conclusion is the same.

Note, however, that up to now tax evasion and unreported labor were assumed away. In countries where earnings test are severe, there is a clear tendency for retirees to get involved in volunteer activities or not to report their earnings. This phenomenon implies that even if earnings tests were desirable, they should be abolished where their yield is negligible and where they are known to lead to inefficient concealments or misallocation of labor time.

Earnings tests and early retirement incentives are two sides of the same reality. In a second-best world in which each individual is subject to an age-dependent nonlinear tax, we would talk of distortions relative to a first-best allocation. There would be no legal age for retirement and no earnings test. Earnings tests appear when there is a statutory age of retirement that could vary based on personal characteristics. With such a statutory age, people who retire before that age are labeled early retirees, and people who are prevented from retiring later because of earnings tests are also early retirees with respect to their undistorted age of retirement.

## 4.8   Conclusion

In this chapter, we introduce the concept of implicit taxation that is widely used in the empirical literature to explain early retirement. We have shown that implicit taxation is partially unavoidable from the viewpoint of social optimality when lump-sum taxes are not available. This is the same argument as the one found in optimal income taxation, where labor supply is reduced for redistributive reasons.

This does not mean that all distortions are desirable. First, for the sake of presentation, we have used linear instruments, even though with nonlinear instruments we could reduce some distortions. For example, the standard "no distortion at the top" is not verified with linear schemes.[12] Second, some of the programs that induce distortions toward early retirement are motivated not by distributive considerations but by either wrong beliefs (early retirement fosters youth employment) or bad fiscal engineering.[13]

Finally, in the above presentation, we assume away private pension arrangements, or rather we assume that they belong to the saving decisions of workers. As already mentioned, some private pension arrangements, particularly the defined-benefit plans, can induce workers to retire earlier than they would otherwise do with social security. In the United States and in Switzerland, for example, it is widely believed that early retirement is in great part due to defined-benefit pensions.

In this chapter, we analyze retirement incentives by focusing on differences in earnings levels and preference for leisure. We have assumed that workers face the same life expectancy. Diamond (2003) extends this analysis to take into account varying life expectancy. He shows that if there is a private annuited market that distinguishes life expectancies, the government should make use of such a market, with the result that overall welfare increases and long-living individuals retire later.

# 5

# The Political Economy of Early Retirement

## 5.1 Introduction

The trend toward earlier and earlier retirement can surely be explained by the steady increase in personal wealth that has permitted workers to enjoy rising living standards, even as they spend a growing percentage of their lives outside the paid workforce. The expansion of a variety of public policies, including social security and private institutions, has over recent decades become an even more important explanation for early retirement. As already alluded to, these policies have been developed to fulfill objectives pertaining to redistribution and employment—objectives that have received wide popular support.

We would like to understand how such support arises. More explicitly, how can we explain the development of policies that clearly discourage work among older individuals and lead to retirement patterns that are too early from most views of social desirability? In this chapter, we deal with this question and its corollary: why is it so difficult to reverse the trend toward early retirement? We first use the standard majority voting approach to determine the political equilibrium value of the age of retirement. We then turn to the limits of such an approach, particularly regarding the difficulty of adopting reforms that can be supported by a wide majority of citizens. We also suggest alternative approaches.

Note that we are not presenting the literature devoted to the collective choice of social security. Most of that literature assumes a fixed age of retirement and is concerned with the determination of payroll-tax and benefit levels.[1]

## 5.2  Political Unpopularity

Although it might seem optimal to raise the retirement age to meet financing problems and improvements in longevity, that logic has so far escaped the general public. In Europe and North America, voters and workers routinely reject the idea of a higher retirement age. Jacobs and Shapiro (1998) summarized the findings of 18 polls that asked Americans about their attitudes toward an increase in retirement age. The polls were conducted over a 20-year period ending in 1997. With rare exceptions, solid majorities of respondents reject any proposed hike in the retirement age. Further, the size of the majority opposing a higher retirement age was higher in the 1990s than it was in the 1980s. The hostility of Americans to reforms is not restricted to a higher retirement age but applies to other basic steps that would solve public pensions' long-term funding problems.

The same holds in almost all European countries where wide majorities are against higher payroll taxes, lower benefits, and a higher retirement age. They basically favor the status quo. In a 10-year-old survey, the so-called Eurobarometer, an interesting question was asked about continuing the existing system even at the cost of requiring higher contributions or contracting the welfare state to a limited number of essential benefits. According to Ferrera (1993), the "continuists" clearly outnumbered the "contractionists" in all the European countries (EC 12). And he concluded that "the legitimacy of social protection in its current format remains robust within the EC as a whole."[2]

On the question of reforming the pension system because of aging, hardly a third of the respondents thought that raising the retirement age was a likely policy option. Germany (45 percent), France (42 percent), and the Netherlands (48 percent) seemed more convinced than the others about the wisdom of raising the pension age.

In a recent survey conducted in Belgium in the Flemish community, people were asked about their preferred retirement age. The majority of respondents cited the age of 57, which is also the effective retirement age and well below the statutory age of 65 (which is known not to be sustainable) (see Schokkaert, Verhue, and Peppermans, 1999).

There are also the surveys on the welfare state by Boeri, Börsch-Supan, and Tabellini (2000, 2002) conducted in Germany, France, Italy, and Spain. They paint the same picture as the earlier Eurobarometer: a majority of citizens does not want any rolling back of the welfare state,

**Table 5.1**
Desired and expected retirement ages in France and Belgium

| France | | | Belgium | | |
|---|---|---|---|---|---|
| Age Class | Desired | Expected | Age Class | Desired | Expected |
| 18–34 | 54.3 | 62.2 | <25 | 55 | 60 |
| 50–64 | 56.4 | 60.3 | >50 | 59 | 60 |

*Source:* Assous (2001); De Vits (2002).

which does not mean that they are happy with the existing programs. Fortunately, the door is not completely closed to reform. A majority of respondents are also in favor of some sort of flexibility in the way in which social security is organized.

In the Eurobarometer of 2002, a couple of questions were asked concerning retirement age. Most Europeans intend to retire between 56 and 60, and very few expect to be still active after age 65. To the question of raising the statutory pensionable age, fewer than a quarter of Europeans (EU 15) would support such a move.[3]

Finally, two surveys were conducted recently in France and Belgium on the desired and expected ages of retirement. In both countries, as shown in table 5.1, young workers would like to retire even earlier than today (58) but expect that this will not be possible. Older workers also desire to retire at an earlier age than either the effective age or their expected age. Note, however, that older workers have a narrower gap between desired and expected ages of retirement than younger ones do.

Political leaders apparently take their cue from these polling numbers. Nearly all the candidates to (presidential or parliamentary) elections have consistently been cautious regarding the idea of a higher retirement age.

In chapter 8, we deal with the belief that early retirement fosters youth employment. We show that this belief is ill-founded. Yet beliefs can be stronger than facts in shaping economic policies. The 2002 Eurobarometer addressed this question. Answers are given in figure 5.1, which shows that in 9 out of 15 European Union countries more than half of the population believes that by exiting the labor force elderly workers help young and unemployed workers. Countries where this perception is particularly strong belong to the southern part of Europe and are among those where early retirement is pervasive and reforms are strongly opposed.[4]

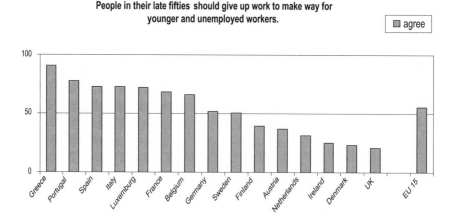

**Figure 5.1**
Perceived intergenerational redistribution
*Source:* European Commission (2003).

## 5.3 The Political Selection of a Retirement Age

As we have seen, the effective age of retirement results from a complex package of taxes, benefits, and eligibility ages. There is no uniform mandatory retirement age. Attempting to model the political choice reveals that the complexity of existing systems results in two distinctive and complementary approaches. In the first one, workers vote on a mandatory age of retirement. In the second one, they vote on something that reflects the implicit tax on postponed activity. This section is devoted to the first approach.

Our model is the standard overlapping two-generations model wherein individuals differ in two respects—their age (first or second period) and their productivity $w^i$. The lifetime utility of an individual of productivity $w_i$ is

$$u^i = u(c^i, d^i, z^i) = u(c^i) + \beta u(d^i - (z^i)^2/2),$$

where $c^i, d^i$, and $z^i$ are, respectively, first- and second-period consumption and the age of retirement. Note that each period consists of one unit of time, $1 + z^i$ is the length of active life, and $z^i$ is the retirement age.

We introduce a pension system that provides benefits that are flat for a fraction $\alpha$ and contributory for a fraction $(1 - \alpha)$. Thus, the pension benefit expected by a worker of productivity $w^i$ is

$$P^i = (1 - \alpha)\tau(1 + n + z^i)w^i + \alpha\tau((1 + n)\overline{w} + \overline{zw}),$$

where $\tau$ is the payroll tax, which is assumed to be the same in both periods and $\overline{zw} = Ezw$. We assume that type $i$ individuals save $s^i(\geq 0)$, which generates an interest income $Rs^i$, where $R \geq 1 + n$. We can now write the individual budget constraints:

$$c^i = w^i(1 - \tau) - s^i$$

$$d^i = Rs^i + w^i(1 - \tau)z^i + p^i$$

$$= Rs^i + w^i(1 - \alpha\tau)z^i + \tau(1 + n)\overline{w} + \alpha\tau\overline{zw}.$$

If workers were free to choose any values for $z^i$, they would choose

$$z^i = (1 - \alpha\tau)w^i$$

and then

$$\overline{wz} = (1 - \alpha\tau)E(w^i)^2.$$

For the time being, we assume that there is no liquidity constraint, which means that for any individual saving $s^{*i}$ is defined by

$$u'(c^i) = \beta Ru'(d^i).$$

Let us now consider a policy of mandatory retirement $\hat{z}$ and first look at the optimal $\hat{z}$ for a young and an old worker of type $i$. We start with a young worker with productivity $w^i$. Given $\tau = \bar{\tau}$, he will choose the value of $\hat{z}^{yi}$ that maximizes

$$u(w^i(1 - \bar{\tau}) - s^i) + \beta u(Rs^i + w^i(1 - \alpha\bar{\tau})\hat{z}^i - (\hat{z}^i)^2/2$$

$$+ \bar{\tau}(1 + n)\overline{w} + \alpha\bar{\tau}z^i\overline{w}).$$

This yields the first-order condition

$$\beta u'(d^i)(w^i(1 - \alpha\bar{\tau}) - \hat{z}^i + \alpha\bar{\tau}\overline{w}) = 0.$$

Henceforth,

$$\hat{z}^{yi} = w^i - \bar{\tau}\alpha(w^i - \overline{w}).$$

The same solution holds true if we look for the optimal choice of an old worker. In other words,

$$\hat{z}^{yi} = \hat{z}^{0i}.$$

This means that the majority choice will be that of the worker, young or old, with median productivity. This solution can be contrasted with that chosen by a utilitarian social planner. Denoting it by $\hat{z}_u$, it is

$$\hat{z}_u = \frac{Eu'(d^i)(w^i - \alpha\bar{\tau}(w^i - \bar{w}))}{Eu'(d^i)}.$$

This is to be compared with the choice of the median worker:

$$\hat{z}_m = w_m - \alpha\bar{\tau}(w_m - \bar{w}).$$

Without more information, it is not possible to know whether $\hat{z}_u \gtrless \hat{z}_m$. Given that $w_m < \bar{w}$, $\hat{z}_u$ is clearly higher than $\hat{z}_m$, with $u(d^i)$ close to linear.

This rather ambiguous conclusion holds true for a defined-contribution rate. If instead we assume defined benefits, the conclusion would be

$$\hat{z}_m^0 < \hat{z}_m^y \gtrless \hat{z}_u.$$

This result is demonstrated in the appendix to this chapter. We now turn to the next point—the choice of the implicit tax.

### 5.4   Determining the Contribution Rate

To keep the analysis relatively simple, we assume that $\alpha = 0$. In other words, the social security system at hand is Beveridgean. In this setting, we look for the optimal payroll tax rate from the viewpoint of each individual, old and young, and ultimately of that of the decisive voter.

The utility of a young worker of type $i$ is

$$u^i = u(w^i(1 - \tau) - s^i)$$

$$+ \beta u\left(s^i R + \frac{(w^i)^2(1 - \tau)^2}{2} + \tau\bar{w}(1 + n) + \tau(1 - \tau)Ew^2\right),$$

and the optimal $\tau^{yi}$ is given by

$$\frac{\partial u^i}{\partial \tau^i} = -\beta u'(d^i)[w^i(R + w^i(1 - \tau)) - \bar{w}(1 + n) - (1 - 2\tau)Ew^2]. \tag{5.1}$$

As to the optimal $\tau^{0i}$, it is given by

$$\frac{\partial u(d^i)}{\partial \tau^i} = -\beta u'(d^i)[(w^i)^2(1 - \tau) - \bar{w}(1 + n) - (1 - 2\tau)Ew^2]. \tag{5.2}$$

One sees right away that $1 \geq \tau^{0i} \geq \tau^{yi} \geq 0$. Under some plausible assumptions, it can be shown that $\tau^{0i} = 1$ for all $i$ and that $\partial \tau^{yi}/\partial w^i < 0$ up to a value of $w^i$ for which $\tau^{yi} = 0$. To get $\tau^{0i} = 1$ for all $i$, we have to assume that even the most productive workers with productivity $w_+$ get more utility with $\tau = 1$ than with $\tau = 0$. In other words, one needs $w_+^2/2$ (the net gain from working in the second period without tax) to be lower than $\overline{w}(1 + n)$ (the flat-rate pension benefit).

It is also easy to show that $\tau_i^0 = 0$ for all workers with productivity $w_i > \tilde{w}_i$, where $\tilde{w}_i$ is defined by

$$\tilde{w}(1 + n) - w^i R + Ew^2 - (w^i)^2 = 0.$$

If $1 + n = R$, $\tilde{w}^i > \overline{w} > w_m$.

As a consequence, if both old and young workers vote on $\tau$, the decisive voter is a young worker with productivity $\tilde{\tilde{w}}$, such that all the old workers plus young workers with productivity below $\tilde{\tilde{w}}$ make up half the population. If only the young workers vote, the decisive voter is the one with median productivity $w_m$ ($\overline{w} > w_m > \tilde{\tilde{w}}$), and he will choose a lower rate of payroll taxation than the worker with productivity $\tilde{\tilde{w}}$.

Finally, let us see the payroll tax that a utilitarian social planner would choose. Its objective would be to maximize

$$E[u(w^i(1 - \tau) - s^i) + \beta u(s^i R + (w^i)^2(1 - \tau)^2/2$$

$$+ \ \tau\overline{w}(1 + n) + (\tau - \tau^2)Ew^2)].$$

The first-order condition is given by

$$E\beta u'(d)[wR + w^2(1 - \tau) - \overline{w}(1 + n) - (1 - 2\tau)Ew^2] = 0. \tag{5.3}$$

Comparing (5.1) and (5.3) does not give a clear indication of the relative value of $\tau$ that is chosen by the majority of young workers and that results from welfare maximization. In contrast, it is quite clear that when both old and young workers vote on $\tau$, they choose a value of $\tau$ higher than the one chosen by the social planner.

All of the above results are summarized in table 5.2. What seems crucial is not the contrast between majority voting and welfare maximization but rather the people who are asked to vote. When both old and young workers vote, there is most often a bias toward early retirement. The reason is simple: in this particular case, the viewpoint of the retirees is twice taken into account—totally by the old workers and partially by the young workers, particularly those with low productivity.

**Table 5.2**
Summary table

| Choice | Utilitarian Solution | Majority of Both Old and Young Workers | Majority of Young Workers |
|---|---|---|---|
| $z$ for given $\tau$ | $\gtreqless$ | | $=$ |
| $z$ for given $p$ | $\gtreqless$ | | $<$ |
| $\tau$ | $\gtreqless$ | | $>$ |
| and thus | | | |
| $z(\tau)$ | $\gtreqless$ | | $<$ |

## 5.5   The Double Dividend of Postponing Retirement

In this section, we argue that one reason that reforms are difficult is a misunderstanding of what the real alternatives are.[5] When asked to vote for or against postponed retirement, people tend to pick the wrong counterfactual. To use an analogy, workers who are asked to choose between a 40-hour work week versus a 35-hour work week, at the same *weekly* income, will choose the shorter work week. On the other hand, if they have to choose between the two work weeks at the same *hourly* wage, then the outcome is far less obvious. A preference for the longer work week then cannot be ruled out.

Often when people are asked to choose between the status quo in terms of benefits and retirement age and a new regime with postponed retirement and similar benefits (yearly pension), they will most likely choose the status quo. This is individually rational. However, this decision is based on an unrealistic alternative. As the dependency rate reaches its peak in a couple of decades, benefits will have to be cut if both contributions and retirement do not change. This is the iron law of pay-as-you-go systems. There was a time when one could escape this iron law by shifting the financial burden to future generations. But today this is less and less possible.

The correct counterfactual is not an unconstrained status quo but a constrained one with a constant retirement pattern but fewer benefits. To make the two situations comparable, we must realize that the unconstrained status quo is unrealistic: benefits have to be cut by an amount equal to the additional revenue generated by postponing the age of retirement.

Following the methodology applied in the National Bureau of Economic Research's (NBER) International Social Security Project, we

**Table 5.3**
Average retirement age

| Income Quintile | Baseline (age) | Reform 1 (age) | Variation (years) |
|---|---|---|---|
| 1 | 57.7 | 60.3 | 2.6 |
| 2 | 57.4 | 60.2 | 2.8 |
| 3 | 57.6 | 60.5 | 2.9 |
| 4 | 58.3 | 61.4 | 3.1 |
| 5 | 59.6 | 62.7 | 3.1 |

consider for the case of Belgium a reform under which the various stat-utory ages of retirement are increased by three years.[6] In Belgium, the normal retirement age is 65. The early entitlement retirement age is 60, which basically means that workers can draw benefits at 60 and that these benefits are full if workers have had a complete career. Increasing these two ages by three years does not mean that all workers will retire three years later. The retirement decision is surely influenced by the reform but also by other considerations, such as the other parameters of the system, their health, their spouse's income, and so on.

Now we look at the impact of such a reform on the lifetime dispos-able income of a cohort of workers age 50, starting from that age until the end of their life. Table 5.3 shows the increase in effective retirement age due to this reform (labeled *reform 1*). It concerns both men and women and five income classes. The average variation is 2.9 years.

Reform 1 will save a certain amount of money due to the increase in social security contributions and to the reduction in the length of benefits payment. (The other taxes are not taken into account in this exercise.) This amount could be used to finance aging and can be expressed as the percentage of the sum of retirement benefits. In our case, the saving is equal to 21.32 percent of retirement benefits. We now compare this scenario to one without reform but with a budget re-duction of 21.32 percent. This budget reduction can be obtained by a uniform reduction of 21.32 percent of retirement benefits. This scenario is called *reform 0*. Now we compare the redistributive impact of these two reforms on the income distribution.

To measure this impact, we take the number of individuals who are under the poverty line, the poverty line being 50 percent of the median income in the baseline. We also take 60 percent of the median income in the baseline. Table 5.4 shows that the number of individuals under

**Table 5.4**
Percentage of individuals under the poverty line

| Income (percentage of median income) | Baseline | Reform 0 | Reform 1 |
| --- | --- | --- | --- |
| 50 | 4.42 | 7.95 | 4.48 |
| 60 | 10.09 | 16.21 | 8.96 |

these two poverty lines does not increase under reform 1, whereas it does increase largely under reform 0.

This empirical exercise is in the spirit of the theoretical model that is shown in equation (4.5), wherein the tax rates would have been equal in the two periods. If the distortions are strong and the pension system very redistributive, it is clear that by restructuring the tax system (higher tax rate in the first period, lower in the second) social welfare can increase, and the utility of low-productivity individuals can increase.

There are clear differences between a theoretical approach and our empirical findings. Our theoretical model is simplistic. The tax-benefit schedule is linear. There is a lot of monotonicity among the individual characteristics (productivity and health), the implicit tax, the level of benefits, and the age of retirement. The welfare of individuals is expressed in terms of utility. By contrast, our empirical model is an intricate black box with actual individuals and actual institutions; it sometimes yields surprising results because no relationship is monotonic. Questions such as marital status, completeness of the work career, and type of occupation matter a lot. Furthermore, our welfare indicator is lifetime income and not utility. In other words, the disutility of working one more year is not taken into account.

## 5.6   Resistance to Socially Desirable Reforms

In the previous section, we argue that resistance to reform can arise from a misunderstanding of alternatives offered to voters. Another reason that desirable reforms can be rejected by a majority, even though it is clear that a majority will benefit from it, is related to the uncertainty regarding winners and losers.[7] To illustrate this point, we keep the simple model used so far. Individual utility is written as

$$u(c, d, z) = u(c) + \beta u(x - z^2/2\gamma),$$

where $c = w(1 - \tau) - s$, $x = w(1 - \tau)z + p + Rs$ and $d = x - z^2/2\gamma$. Without liquidity constraint, $s^*$ is defined by

$$-u'(c) + u'(d)\beta R = 0,$$

and without constraint on retirement, it is defined by

$$z^* = \gamma w(1 - \tau).$$

We consider a society consisting of three groups of individuals: group 1 has low productivity $w_L$ and bad health $\gamma_L$; group 2 has low productivity $w_L$ and good health $\gamma_H(>\gamma_L)$; and group 3 has high productivity $w_H(>w_L)$ and good health $\gamma_H$. The proportion of individuals of type $i$ is $\pi_i$.[8]

At the start, we have a pension system with given $\tau$, a uniform pension, and a mandatory age of retirement $\bar{z}$, such that

$$z_1^* < \bar{z} < z_2^* < z_3^*.$$

The pension benefit is equal to

$$p = \tau\bar{w}[(1 + n) + \bar{z}].$$

In such a setting, type 1 individuals would like to work fewer years, and individuals of types 2 and 3 would like to work more years.

Consider a reform that increases the mandatory age $\bar{z}$ while respecting the revenue constraint. In other words,

$$p' = \tau\bar{w}[(1 + n) + \bar{z}'],$$

where the primes denote the postreform values. We assume that $s^*$ does not change. Quite clearly, individuals of types 2 and 3 will gain. Individuals of type 1 can lose if the disutility of working longer offsets the financial gains: $w_L\Delta\bar{z} + \Delta p$. One can show that they indeed lose if

$$\tau\bar{w}\Delta\bar{z} + w_L(1 + \tau)\Delta\bar{z} - (\bar{z} + \Delta\bar{z})^2/2\gamma + \bar{z}^2/\gamma < 0$$

or

$$(\tau\bar{w} + w_L(1 + \tau)) - \Delta\bar{z}/2\gamma - \bar{z}/\gamma < 0.$$

We assume that this is the case. Even though $\Delta u_1 < 0$, we assume that the overall social welfare increases:

$$\pi_1\Delta u_1 + \pi_2\Delta u_2 + \pi_3\Delta u_3 > 0.$$

Then the reform is socially desirable. Further, if $\pi_2 + \pi_3 > 1/2$, then a majority benefits from the reform.

Suppose now that before voting for the reform, individuals of types 1 and 2 are indistinguishable from each other because they do not know their real health status. Disability will come later, and the only thing they know is that they have a probability $\pi_1/(\pi_1 + \pi_2)$ of being disabled (that is, having $\gamma_L$). If $\pi_1 \Delta u_1 + \pi_2 \Delta u_2 > 0$ and $\pi_1 + \pi_2 > 1/2$, then a majority will oppose the reform.

This is an illustration of why an apparently desirable reform can be rejected. Any government that understands the underlying mechanism of this model will make sure that a disability insurance protects those who are unlucky. But this requires good information, and we have already shown that one of the main problems of social policy is informational asymmetry. This also requires trust in government's promises.

## 5.7 Conclusion

Surveys and political events show clearly that people are attached to the current pensionable age and resist most attempts to raise it. Their behavior shows that they do not seem to be concerned by the challenge of demographic aging or by the issue of financial sustainability.

What can we do about the fact that some countries have a social security system that induces people to retire early and find it difficult to reform that system, even when reform would clearly be welfare enhancing? We need to better inform and include future generations in the reform process. Better information about the cost and unsustainability of current public pension systems can help obtain support for reforms that raise the retirement age and modify the benefit structure. Yet information alone is insufficient if a majority of voters thinks that they would lose with the reform, even though future generations would gain far more than voters would lose. Widespread altruism might lead to a change in thinking, but if not, the public authority has a duty to force the decision.

One of the main reasons for a distortion toward early retirement is that when the whole population participates in the electoral process, retirees vote twice—as retirees and as young workers who are future retirees. When the vote is restricted to just the young, the outcome is closer to the socially optimal solution obtained by focusing on the lifetime utility of a generation. This observation should not be perceived as intending to exclude the elderly from a decision that concerns them.

For programs that involve intergenerational transfers and thus the possibility of burdening future generations, the most reasonable approach is to vote behind the veil of ignorance, with a generational viewpoint, and without knowing which generation one belongs to.

In this chapter, we have exclusively used the simple majority model. Other approaches include one that is based on pressure groups. For example, Mulligan and Sala-i-Martin (1999) introduce a time-intensive political competition between two interest groups—a young generation and an old generation. To create a lobbying-inducing activity, pressure groups have to favor activities that discourage their members from working. Groups whose members work less are more homogeneous with regard to their objectives, and they are thus more effective in getting transfers. This competition turns out to be favorable to the old generation, which has more free time and is more focused on narrow self-interest issues. This approach thus provides a different explanation for early retirement.

## 5.8 Appendix

In this appendix, we look at the determination of retirement age $z^i$, given the benefits. The benefits are Beveridgean. We thus assume that the $P^{i\prime}$s are fixed and equal to $\bar{P}$ with

$$\bar{P} = \tau(1 + n + z)\bar{w}.$$

This implies

$$\tau = \tau(z) = \frac{\bar{P}}{(1 + n + z)\bar{w}}$$

and $\quad \tau' = \tau'(z) = -\dfrac{\tau}{1 + n + z}.$

• Choice of the young workers: We want to know the most preferred retirement age $z^i$ of young workers with productivity $w^i$. Each solves the following problem:

$$Max_{z,s} \; u(w^i(1 - \tau(z)) - s^i) + \beta u(Rs^i + \bar{P} + w^i(1 - \tau(z))z - z^2/2).$$

We derive the following two first-order conditions:

$$-u'(c^i) + \beta R u'(d^i) = 0$$

$$-u'(c^i)w_i\tau'(z) - \beta u'(d^i)[w^i\tau'(z)z - w^i(1 - \tau) - z] = 0.$$

Combining these two conditions, we obtain

$$-w^i \tau'(z)(R+z) + w^i(1-\tau) - z = 0$$

or

$$\frac{\tau w^i(R+z)}{1+n+z} + w^i(1-\tau) - z = 0.$$

• Choice of the old workers:

$$\frac{\tau w^i z}{1+n+z} + w^i(1-\tau) - z = 0.$$

Clearly, old workers are in favor of a lower age of retirement than young workers.

• Social-welfare maximization:

$$Max_z \ E\{u(w(1-\tau(z)) - s) + \beta u(Rs + \bar{P} + w(1-\tau(z))z - z^2/2)]$$

The first-order condition is given as:

$$E\{u'(c)(-\tau'(z))w + \beta u'(d)[(z(-\tau'(z))w) + w(1-\tau) - z] = 0$$

or

$$\beta E u'(d)\left[(R+z)\frac{\tau w}{1+n+z} + w(1-\tau) - z\right] = 0.$$

For $u(\cdot)$ not very concave and a large gap between the median and the average wage, the value of $z$ chosen by the majority of the young is expected to be lower than the value of $z$ maximizing social welfare. If instead $u(\cdot)$ is very concave, we have the reverse. Assume, for example, an extreme concavity leading to the Rawlsian criterion. Then the optimal $z$ will be very low—lower than that chosen by the majority of young workers or even the majority of all individuals alive.

# 6

# An Overlapping-Generations Model with Retirement and Taxation

## 6.1 Introduction

Much of the theoretical discussion of the economics of pension refers to the overlapping-generations model that was developed by Samuelson (1958) and Diamond (1965).[1] The alleged depressing effect of pay-as-you-go (PAYG) schemes on savings, the consequences of aging on the financial viability of social security, and the shift from PAYG to fully funded (FF) schemes are three examples that are often addressed. In these studies, the age of retirement generally is taken as given, and the source of financing is a payroll tax.[2]

Yet we know from recent studies that there can be a negative interaction between the age of retirement and the financing of pensions. Payroll taxes imply a downward distortion of the labor participation of elderly workers, which in turn increases the dependency ratio and hence the financing problems of social security. One thus looks for alternative sources of financing, such as consumption and capital income taxation.

This chapter extends the canonical overlapping-generations model in two directions—by allowing for a variable retirement age and by considering the optimal mix between labor income and capital income taxation. Since one of the features of the overlapping-generations model is that the market solution can be inefficient and not generally socially optimal, we consider the possibility of debt policy to achieve an optimal intergenerational reallocation of resources. Throughout this chapter, we assume that social security benefits are provided, given the fact that most advanced-economy governments are committed to providing the elderly with replacement income.

Our approach is related to the approaches of Hu (1979) and Atkinson and Sandmo (1980). It builds on the standard overlapping-generations model. Individuals are assumed to live for two periods

—consuming in both, inelastically providing a unit of labor in the first one, and making an endogenous labor-supply decision in the second. This decision is interpreted as the timing of retirement. It is an idea similar to Hu's with the difference that we consider a richer set of policy instruments.[3] Like Atkinson and Sandmo, we introduce two tax instruments—an interest income tax and a labor income tax. But we make labor supply endogenous in the second rather than first period of life. Like them, we show that the optimal tax structure depends on whether debt policy is available. When it is not, our tax instruments are used not only to finance social security benefits and other fixed public spending with allocative distortions but also to improve the intergenerational allocation of resources.

The main message of this chapter is that when the government lacks nondistortionary instruments, except for public debt, it is expected to impose a positive tax on wage income and interest income and implicitly encourage early retirement.[4] If the age of retirement is very sensitive to taxation, then more reliance on interest income tax would be expected. When debt policy is not available and there is underaccumulation at the start, the payroll tax will be lower than it would be were public debt available.

We begin our analysis by presenting the overlapping-generations model with a variable retirement age and tax and debt instruments. Then we turn to the laissez-faire equilibrium and first-best optimality conditions. We also indicate under what conditions the first-best allocation can be decentralized. These conditions are public debt to achieve the modified golden rule and lump-sum taxation to finance social security benefits and other public spending. Next, we turn to the case when lump-sum taxation is not available, and we derive the second-best tax structure with or without public debt. The chapter concludes with a short summary of the main findings and a discussion of key assumptions.

Unlike in the two previous chapters, here individuals are identical. The focus is on the dynamic aspects and specifically on the well-known and yet paradoxical finding that retiring early forces individuals to save and leads to a high level of consumption. With the life-cycle saving hypothesis, working too long can be a liability. The approach is one of general equilibrium with endogenous factor prices. It also makes clear that in a dynamic setting taxes and transfers affect the distribution of utilities at one time but also affect capital accumulation and thus welfare in the long term.

## 6.2   The Model

### 6.2.1   *Households*

The model is that of overlapping generations and life-cycle savings with a variable retirement age. People live for two periods of unitary length. Members of generation $t$ consume $c_t$ in period $t$ and supply a unit of labor. In period $t+1$, they consume $d_{t+1}$ and work a fraction $z_{t+1}$ of that period. The variable $z_{t+1}$ can also be interpreted as the retirement age of members of generation $t$.

Individuals maximize an identical utility function with standard properties (strictly concave, continuously differentiable, and fulfilling Inada conditions)[5]:

$$u_t = u(c_t, d_{t+1}, 1 - z_{t+1}).$$

We assume a pay-as-you-go pension system with fixed benefits $(P_t)_{t\geq 0}$. Pensions can be financed in the same period that they are paid by a number of tax instruments—a lump-sum tax in the first period of life $a_t$; a proportional wage tax $\tau_{wt}$; a tax on capital income $\tau_{rt}$.[6]

In the first period of life, each individual faces the budget constraint

$$c_t + s_t = (1 - \tau_{wt})w_t - a_t, \tag{6.1}$$

where $s_t$ denotes savings and $w_t$ the wage rate. In the second period, the individual faces the constraint

$$d_{t+1} = (1 + (1 - \tau_{rt+1})r_{t+1})s_t + (1 - \tau_{wt+1})w_{t+1}z_{t+1} + P_{t+1}, \tag{6.2}$$

where $r_{t+1}$ is the rate of interest.

These two constraints are merged to yield a life-cycle budget constraint

$$c_t + q_{t+1}d_{t+1} = \omega_t - a_t + q_{t+1}\omega_{t+1}z_{t+1} + q_{t+1}P_{t+1}, \tag{6.3}$$

where $q_{t+1} = (1 + (1 - \tau_{rt+1})r_{t+1})^{-1}$ and $\omega_t = (1 - \tau_{wt})w_t$.

Maximizing $u_t$ subject to (6.3) yields the first-order conditions

$$u'_{d_{t+1}} - q_{t+1}u'_{c_t} = 0 \tag{6.4}$$

and

$$u'_{1-z_{t+1}} - \omega_{t+1}u'_{d_{t+1}} \geq 0 \quad (= 0 \text{ if } z_{t+1} > 0). \tag{6.5}$$

Accordingly, the optimal choices of $c_t$, $d_{t+1}$, and $z_{t+1}$ depend on the vector $X_t = (\omega_t - a_t, \omega_{t+1}, q_{t+1}, \bar{p}_{t+1})$. This gives the indirect utility function

$$v_t = v(X_t) = u(c(X_t), d(X_t), 1 - z(X_t)).$$

Note that the first argument is a lump-sum income, while the second is a price argument. To make this distinction clear, we use the notation $\omega_{0t} (= w_t - a_t)$, where the wage has a nondistortionary effect.

Henceforth, we write $\partial c_t / \partial \omega_{0t}$ for the income effect and $\partial c_t / \partial \omega_{t+1}$ for the price effect.

Saving is given by

$$s_t = \omega_t - a_t - c(X_t) = s(X_t). \tag{6.6}$$

Each generation $t$ consists of $N_t$ individuals with $N_t = N_{t-1}(1 + n)$. Total population in time $t$ is thus equal to $N_t + N_{t-1}$. In period $t = 0$, there are $N_{-1}$ old agents who hold $s_{-1}$. They choose $d_0$ and $z_0$ subject to constraint

$$d_0 = (1 + (1 - \tau_{r0})r_0)s_{-1} + (1 - \tau_{w0})w_0 z_0 + \bar{p}_0.$$

Their optimal choice is given by (6.5) for $t + 1 = 0$.

### 6.2.2 Production

The production side is assumed to be represented by an aggregate production function relating output $Y_t$ to capital $K_t$ and labor $L_t$:

$$Y_t = F(K_t, L_t),$$

where $F$ is a twice differentiable increasing concave function, homogeneous of degree one. This property means that we can use an intensive form:

$$y_t = F\left(\frac{K_t}{L_t}, 1\right) = f(k_t),$$

with $y = Y/L$ and $k = K/L$.

With perfect competition, factor payments equal the value of marginal products:

$$w_t = F_L(K_t, L_t), \tag{6.7}$$

and

$$1 + r_t = F_K(K_t, L_t),$$ (6.8)

where we assume total depreciation after one period.

### 6.2.3 Government

Government policy includes the taxes introduced above, the pension benefits $\bar{p}_t$, some revenue requirement (public expenditures) $G_t$, and the possibility of public debt $B_t$. We can write the revenue constraint in period $t$ as

$$B_t = (1 + r_t)B_{t-1} + G_t + N_{t-1}\bar{p}_t - N_t a_t - \tau_{wt} w_t (N_t + N_{t-1} z_t)$$

$$- \tau_{rt} r_t N_{t-1} s_{t-1}.$$ (6.9)

We here adopt a comprehensive approach to fiscal policy: the pay-as-you-go social security and the general revenue are integrated. If they were separated, most of the conclusions below would not hold.

## 6.3 Market Equilibrium and First-Best Optimality

### 6.3.1 Intertemporal Equilibrium

We now turn to the intertemporal equilibrium, given the policy instruments just introduced and the initial conditions pertaining to debt $B_{-1}$ and capital stock $K_0$. Each member of generation $-1$ is thus characterized by $s_{-1}$ with

$$s_{-1} = \frac{K_0 + B_{-1}}{N_{-1}}.$$

We define our intertemporal equilibrium as the sequence for prices $(w_t, r_t)_{t \geq 0}$ (implying $\omega_t$ and $q_t$), for individual quantities $(c_t, s_t, d_t, z_t)_{t \geq 0}$, and for aggregate quantities $(K_{t+1}, L_t, Y_t, B_t)_{t \geq 0}$. These verify for $t \geq 0$ the household constraints and optimality conditions (6.1), (6.2), (6.4), and (6.5), as well as profit-maximization conditions (6.7) and (6.8), revenue constraint (6.9), and equilibrium conditions on labor and commodity markets:

$$L_t = N_t + N_{t-1} z_t$$ (6.10)

and

$$F(K_t, L_t) = N_t c_t + N_{t-1} d_t + K_{t+1} + G_t.$$ (6.11)

In Michel and Pestieau (2003), we characterize such an equilibrium. It is worth noting that the government revenue constraint is equivalent to the capital accumulation equation

$$K_{t+1} + B_t = N_t s_t \qquad (6.12)$$

or

$$x_{t+1} + b_t = s_t,$$

where $x_{t+1} = K_{t+1}/N_t$ and $b_t = B_t/N_t$.

### 6.3.2 Optimal Growth

From resource constraints (6.10) and (6.11), we write

$$F(x_t, 1 + n + z_t) = (1 + n)c_t + d_t + (1 + n)x_{t+1} + (1 + n)g_t, \qquad (6.13)$$

where $g_t = G_t/N_t$. To characterize the first-best optimum, we use as the objective pursued by the social planner the sum of lifetime utilities over generations discounted by a factor $\beta$ ($0 < \beta < 1$):

$$\sum_{-1}^{\infty} \beta^t u(c_t, d_{t+1}, 1 - z_{t+1}). \qquad (6.14)$$

The social planner maximizes (6.14) subject to (6.13) and $z_t \geq 0$; $x_0 = K_0/N_{-1}$ and $c_{-1}$ are given. Substituting $d_t = F(x_t, 1 + n + z_t) - (1 + n)(c_t + g_t + x_{t+1})$ in (6.14) and differentiating with respect to $c_t, z_t,$ and $x_{t+1}$ for $t \geq 0$, we obtain

$$\beta u'_{c_t} = (1 + n)u'_{d_t}, \qquad (6.15)$$

$$u'_{1-z_t} \leq u'_{d_t} F_L(x_t, 1 + n + z_t), \ (= \text{if } z_t > 0), \quad \text{and} \qquad (6.16)$$

$$(1 + n)u'_{d_t} = \beta u'_{d_{t+1}} F_K(x_{t+1}, 1 + n + z_{t+1}). \qquad (6.17)$$

Conditions (6.15) and (6.17) imply that

$$u'_{c_t} = u'_{d_{t+1}} F'_K(x_{t+1}, 1 + n + z_{t+1}). \qquad (6.18)$$

We denote the optimal solution obtained from these conditions with $(c_t^*, d_t^*, z_t^*)_{t \geq 0}$ and $(x_t^*)_{t \geq 1}$. We assume that such a solution exists.

It is well known that the market solution can result in either under- or overaccumulation of capital with respect to the (modified) golden rule. Although unnecessary, we make the assumption that the laissez-faire situation results in underaccumulation.

As to the age of retirement, it depends on the various parameters of this economy and, in particular, on what we could call the "taste" for retirement implicit in the individual utility function. In Michel and Pestieau (2000), we show that the laissez-faire capital stock is a decreasing function of the taste for retirement. A society where people tend to work late in life is a society that saves relatively little.

### 6.3.3   Decentralization

We now turn to the problem of decentralization—how to achieve the optimal solution in a market economy by appropriately using some policy instruments.

THEOREM 6.1 (DECENTRALIZATION)   Given a sequence of pension benefits $(P_t)_{t \geq 0}$, there exists a single policy for which the optimal solution is an intertemporal market equilibrium.

This policy consists of not taxing wage earnings ($\tau_{wt} = 0$ for $t \geq 0$) and capital income, except in period 0: $\tau_{rt} = 0$ for $t > 0$ and $\tau_{r0}$, such that[7]

$$d_0^* = (1 + (1 - \tau_{r0})r_0^*)s_{-1} + w_0^* z_0^* + P_0.$$

At each period $t \geq 0$, equilibrium prices are

$$w_t^* = F_L(x_t^*, 1 + n + z_t^*) \quad \text{and} \quad 1 + r_t^* = F_K(x_t^*, 1 + n + z_t^*).$$

Equilibrium saving should verify

$$d_{t+1}^* = (1 + r_{t+1}^*)s_t^* + w_{t+1}^* z_{t+1} + P_{t+1}$$

and optimal debt

$$b_t^* = s_t^* - x_{t+1}^*.$$

These two conditions determine the sequences for $b_t^*$.

Finally, the lump-sum tax $a_t^*$ can be used to ensure that the first-period budget constraint holds:

$$a_t^* = w_t^* - c_t^* - s_t^*.$$

This theorem results from the characteristics of the intertemporal equilibrium. Social optimality verifies both resource constraints and the choices of households given in (6.4) and (6.5) with no distortionary taxes. To fulfill the budget constraints of households at each period, we first use $\tau_{r0}$ and then $(a_t)_{t \geq 0}$ along with debt policy. Alternatively, a pay-as-you-go social security scheme could be used to decentralize the optimum.

### 6.3.4  Steady-State Conditions

In the next section, devoted to the second-best optimum, we consider only the steady-state conditions, first by looking at the decentralization conditions in a steady state. They can be written as

$$\frac{u'_c}{u'_d} = 1 + r^* = F'_K = \frac{1+n}{\beta} \tag{6.19}$$

and

$$\frac{u'_{1-z}}{u'_d} \leq w^* = F_L(x^*, 1+n+z^*) \quad (=0 \text{ if } z^* > 0). \tag{6.20}$$

Equation (6.19), which comes from (6.15) and (6.18), gives the modified golden rule, as well as the condition for the optimal choice of present and future consumption. It implies that $\tau_r = 0$. Equation (6.20), which is equation (6.16) in a steady state, yields the formula for the optimal retirement age: individuals should retire when the marginal utility of the first year of retirement is equal to the marginal productivity of one more year of activity times the marginal utility of consumption. In case of inequality, individuals should retire at the beginning of the second period. Equation (6.20) implies that $\tau_w = 0$.

We now turn to the revenue constraint in a steady state with $\tau_w = \tau_r = 0$:

$$b^*(1+n) = b^*(1+r^*) + g(1+n) + P - a^*(1+n)$$

or

$$b^* \frac{1-\beta}{\beta} + g + \frac{P}{1+n} - a^* = 0 \tag{6.21}$$

using $1 + r^* = (1+n)/\beta$ from (6.19).

### 6.4  Second-Best Policy

In general, lump-sum taxation such as $a_t$ is not available. Unrestricted public debt might even not be possible. Hence, both social security benefits and public spending have to be financed with distortionary taxes on wage and capital income. We now turn to the so-called second-best problem. First, we use a debt policy that ensures that the modified golden rule is satisfied. Then without the debt policy, we see that our tax instruments are to be used to achieve two objectives— dynamic optimality and public-spending financing.

We use the objective function (6.14) with the indirect utility function, and we maximize it with respect to $q_t$, $\omega_t$, and $b_t$, subject to the resource constraint (which is equivalent to the revenue constraint):

$$F(q_t(d_t(X_{t-1}) - \omega_t z_t(X_{t-1}) - \bar{P}_t) - b_{t-1}, 1 + n + z_t(X_{t-1}))$$

$$-d_t(X_{t-1}) + (1+n)b_t - (1+n)\omega_t - (1+n)g_t = 0. \tag{6.22}$$

The problem of the central planner can thus be represented by the Lagrangian function:

$$\mathscr{L} = \sum_{-1}^{\infty} \beta^t \{ v_t(X_t) + \mu_t[F(q_t(d_t(X_{t-1}) - \omega_t z_t(X_{t-1}) - \bar{P}_t) - b_{t-1},$$

$$1 + n + z_t(X_{t-1})) - d_t(X_{t-1}) + (1+n)b_t - (1+n)\omega_t - (1+n)g_t]\},$$

where $\mu$ is the multiplier associated with the resource constraint and $X_t = (\omega_t, \omega_{t+1}, q_{t+1}, \bar{P}_{t+1})$ denotes the arguments of the indirect utility function, the demand function for $d$, and the supply function of $z$. Note that $\bar{P}_{t+1}$ being given cannot be considered as an instrument. The first-order condition can now be written as

$$\frac{\partial \mathscr{L}}{\partial b_t} = -\beta^{t+1}\mu_{t+1}(1 + r_{t+1}) + \beta^t \mu_t(1+n) = 0; \tag{6.23}$$

$$\frac{\partial \mathscr{L}}{\partial q_{t+1}} = -\beta^t u'_{c_t} \frac{s_t}{q_{t+1}} + \beta^{t+1}\mu_{t+1} \left[ \theta_{t+1} \left( \frac{\partial d_{t+1}}{\partial q_{t+1}} - \omega_{t+1} \frac{\partial z_{t+1}}{\partial q_{t+1}} \right) \right.$$

$$\left. + \tau_{wt+1}w_{t+1} \frac{\partial z_{t+1}}{\partial q_{t+1}} + (1 + r_{t+1}) \frac{s_t}{q_{t+1}} \right] = 0; \tag{6.24}$$

$$\frac{\partial \mathscr{L}}{\partial \omega_t} = \beta^t u'_{c_t} + \beta^{t-1} u'_{c_{t+1}} q_t z_t + \beta^t \mu_t \left[ \theta_t \left( \frac{\partial d_t}{\partial \omega_t} - \omega_t \frac{\partial z_t}{\partial \omega_t} - z_t \right) \right.$$

$$\left. + \tau_{wt}w_t \frac{\partial z_t}{\partial \omega_t} - (1 + n + z_t) \right] + \beta^{t+1}\mu_{t+1} \left[ \theta_{t+1} \left( \frac{\partial d_{t+1}}{\partial \omega_{0t}} - \omega_{t+1} \frac{\partial z_{t+1}}{\partial \omega_{0t}} \right) \right.$$

$$\left. + \tau_{wt+1}w_{t+1} \frac{\partial z_{t+1}}{\partial \omega_{0t}} \right] = 0, \tag{6.25}$$

where $\theta_t = \tau_{rt}r_t q_t$. In our interpretation of these conditions, we focus on the steady-state and distinguish two settings, depending on the availability of the debt policy.

Optimal debt policy (6.23) in the steady-state condition leads to the modified golden rule (6.19): $\beta(1+r) = 1 + n < 1 + r$. The steady-state values of $d$ and $z$ are functions of $\omega_0$, $\omega$, and $q$. Combining (6.24) and (6.25), we get

$$\frac{\beta + qz}{-s/q} = \frac{\theta\dfrac{\partial d}{\partial \omega} + \Omega\dfrac{\partial z}{\partial \omega} - (1 + n + z(1 + \theta)) + \beta\left(\theta\dfrac{\partial d}{\partial \omega_0} + \Omega\dfrac{\partial z}{\partial \omega_0}\right)}{\theta\dfrac{\partial d}{\partial q} + \Omega\dfrac{\partial z}{\partial q} + (1 + r)s/q},$$

where $\Omega = \tau_w w - \omega\theta = w(\tau_w - (1 - \tau_w)\theta)$, $\tau_w - (1 - \tau_w)/\theta$ being the net tax rate on second-period activity.

We then use the compensated demand derivatives[8] denoted by a tilde to simplify the above expression. The income effects cancel out, and we are left with

$$-\theta\left[\left(\frac{\partial \tilde{d}}{\partial q} - \omega\frac{\partial \tilde{z}}{\partial q}\right)\frac{\beta + qz}{s/q} + \left(\frac{\partial \tilde{d}}{\partial \omega} - \omega\frac{\partial \tilde{z}}{\partial w}\right)\right]$$

$$= \tau_w w\left[\frac{\partial \tilde{z}}{\partial \omega} + \frac{\partial \tilde{z}}{\partial q}\frac{\beta + qz}{s/q}\right] + \beta(1 + r) - (1 + n). \qquad (6.26)$$

Assume for simplicity's sake that the cross-derivatives are zero. We then have

$$-\theta\left(\frac{\partial \tilde{d}}{\partial q}\frac{\beta + qz}{s/q} - \omega\frac{\partial \tilde{z}}{\partial \omega}\right) = \tau_w w\frac{\partial \tilde{z}}{\partial \omega} + \beta(1 + r) - (1 + n), \qquad (6.27)$$

where $\partial \tilde{z}/\partial \omega > 0$ and $\partial \tilde{d}/\partial q < 0$. This equation characterizes the relative levels of the tax rates on income from labor and capital, with the absolute levels being determined by the revenue requirements of the government.

This characterization depends on compensated derivatives, not on gross derivatives. The absence of income effects is explained by the fact that they are irrelevant for an assessment of the relative merits of different kinds of distortionary taxes.

### 6.4.1 Debt Policy

If debt policy is available, $\beta(1 + r) = (1 + n)$, and we see from (6.27) that

$$\frac{\tau_r r q}{\tau_w w} = \frac{\dfrac{\partial \tilde{z}}{\partial \omega}}{\omega \dfrac{\partial \tilde{z}}{\partial \omega} - \dfrac{\beta + qz}{s/q} \dfrac{\partial \tilde{d}}{\partial q}}. \tag{6.28}$$

If the age of retirement is completely inelastic (along the compensated supply curve), then the optimal tax on interest income is zero, while the tax on earnings is equivalent to a lump-sum tax. On the other hand, if the demand for future consumption is inelastic, then the argument is not reversed, as in Atkinson and Sandmo (1980). It would be reversed if the supply of saving were inelastic—for example, if the denominator of (6.28) was zero. In Atkinson and Sandmo, $s = qd$, whereas here $s = q(d - \omega z - P)$. In other words, saving and second-period consumption do not coincide.

Clearly, the relative tax rates depend on the relative magnitudes of the two derivatives. There is no particular reason to believe that the optimal rates should be the same for the two sources of income or that one of the taxes should be zero. When the relative magnitude of $(\partial \tilde{z}/\partial \omega)/(\partial \tilde{d}/\partial q)$ is high, the relative tax rate $\tau_r/\tau_w$ is low. This interpretation carries over with appropriate modifications to the case of nonzero cross-derivatives. It is a straightforward application of the Ramsey tax rule.

### 6.4.2   No Debt Policy

When there is no optimal debt policy, the modified golden rule is not likely to be satisfied. Suppose there is underaccumulation with respect to the optimal level of saving—namely, $1 + n < \beta(1 + r)$. From (6.27) and given $\partial \tilde{z}/\partial \omega > 0$ and $\partial \tilde{d}/\partial \omega < 0$, we see immediately that the case for an interest income tax is strengthened and the one for an earning tax weakened. This result carries over if the coefficient of $\theta$ is negative and that of $\tau_w w$ is positive—that is, where the direct effects dominate the cross-effects.

In such a case, when the capital intensity of the economy is too low, we would like to encourage saving. To do so, it is desirable to decrease the tax on earning, which implies increasing the tax on interest income because earning is the source of saving. This is clear with a loglinear utility where saving is proportional to first-period earning and independent of the rate of interest. With more general utility, the outcome is likely to be less clear-cut.

### 6.4.3   Interpretation

What does this imply in terms of retirement age? With $g$ and $\bar{P}$ given, $\tau_w$ is most likely to be positive. It will be relatively lower if public borrowing is not available and $1 + n < \beta(1 + r)$. It will also be lower if the derivative of $z$ with respect to net wage is high. In any case, the retirement age will generally be below what it would be in a first-best optimum.

If instead of debt policy, $P$ were allowed to be freely adjusted and financed by a lump-sum tax in the first period, then we would have the modified golden rule with most probably both $P_t$ and $a_t$ as negative.

If the government could control the retirement age $z$, or alternatively if the tax on earnings were used only in the first period of life, then $\tau_w$ would act as a lump-sum tax, and there would be no distortion ($\tau_r = 0$). With a debt policy, the first-best allocation would be obtained.

If the pension system were fully funded ($p = \tau_w w(1 + r + z)$) and $g = 0$, then $\tau_r = 0$ and $\tau_w$ would not be distortionary. With a debt policy, the first-best solution is achieved.

Our model could be extended to an economy with heterogeneous individuals with different productivities. Then with debt policy and a nonlinear tax on earnings, as shown by Stiglitz (1987), $\tau_r = 0$. Evidently a nonlinear tax on earnings acts as a lump-sum tax, making capital income taxation superfluous. However, in our setting, where people work in both periods, individuals' ability in the second period would have to be assumed to be unobservable and independent of ability in the first period.

From equation (6.28), the difference between our result and that of Atkinson and Sandmo is clear. The elasticity of compensated labor supply with respect to wage taxation has two effects: a direct effect on earnings in the numerator and an indirect effect on savings in the denominator. The first effect discourages taxation of earnings; the second one encourages it (fewer earnings in the second period means more savings). This second effect does not appear in Atkinson and Sandmo but is clearly dominated by the first one.

### 6.5   Conclusions

The purpose of this chapter has been to extend Diamond's (1965) overlapping-generations model with social security in two directions—by endogenizing the choice of the age of retirement and by considering two distortionary taxes on capital and labor income. In so doing, we have incorporated the contributions of Atkinson and Sandmo (1980) to the optimal taxation of earnings and savings and the contributions of Hu (1979) to the study of social security with endogenous retirement.

As in any optimal taxation model, our conclusions are sensitive to the assumptions made concerning the range of instruments that are available to the government. If the government pursues an independent debt policy, it can always obtain the modified golden rule path so that we obtain a standard Ramsey tax structure. On the other hand, if the government uses a nondistortionary payroll tax or a nonlinear income tax (with many individuals differing in productivity and separability between consumption and retirement) along with debt policy, then an interest income tax does not have to be used.

In general, however, it is reasonable to believe that both kinds of taxes are needed. Particularly when the revenue requirement (social security benefits and public spending) is high, the tax on earnings is positive, thus generating a bias toward early retirement. This tax will be less important if the relative magnitude of the price derivative of retirement age is high or if there is an underaccumulation of capital.

A number of studies have shown that the observed decline in the rate of participation of elderly workers in the labor market is due to the implicit marginal tax rate that social security imposes on working one additional year. In this chapter, we show that, given the range of instruments that are available to the government, such an incentive to early retirement is unavoidable. We also show that this distortion can be partially alleviated by a tax on interest income.

# 7    Disability Insurance

## 7.1   Introduction

The trend toward a generalized decrease in retirement entry age is a
significant problem. The dominant explanation for this trend is implicit
taxation on the continued activity of elderly workers. This argument
assumes that workers have, individually or collectively, a large degree
of discretion concerning retirement age.[1]

Some early retirement decisions result from the deliberate policies of
decision makers, such as early retirement schemes in some declining
industries, disability insurance for disabled workers, and unemployment insurance for workers who have no chance to find another job. It
may be that policymakers have used too many of these policies in com-
plicity with unions and management. It also may be that some programs have been diverted from their original purpose. For example,
unemployment insurance and disability insurance have at times been
used not only to compensate for "genuine" unemployment or disability but also to allow healthy and still productive workers to withdraw
from the labor force. The data on disability (for unemployment, the issue is trickier) do not encompass only disabled workers; they also include people who want to stop working to benefit from a system with
loose controls.

Such "flaws" in control may be deliberate or not. They may certainly
be an effect of bad policy design. However, it is not clear that a system-
atic use of tight controls on everyone who applies for, say, disability
benefits is necessarily the appropriate policy. The question is where to
draw the line between disability benefits (which would be subject to
more or less tight screening) and (early) retirement benefits (which are
conditional on age and on the individual's retirement decision).

This is one of the questions discussed in this chapter. We show that without controls a number of workers who value leisure highly will use disability insurance as a way to leave the labor market. Such behavior results in a relatively low age of retirement and a relatively low level of disability benefits. Accordingly, we introduce the possibility of controls that sort out disabled workers from healthy but retirement-prone workers. We show that such controls can increase both social welfare and the rate of participation of elderly workers and can help disabled workers be better taken care of. At the same time, we also show that it is not optimal to test all applicants or to apply testing to all types of benefits.

To address these issues, we use a simple model with three different types of individuals with identical productivity: hard-working individuals, retirement-prone individuals, and disabled individuals. At first sight, the last two types appear to be similar because both disabled individuals and retirement-prone individuals have a high disutility of labor—the former because effort hurts them and the latter because they like leisure. Thus, the social planner would like to give more weight to the disabled individual relative to the hard-working and retirement-prone (from here on called lazy) workers. Yet if the lazy cannot be differentiated from the disabled, they will be given the same package (or at least the same utility level).

We introduce an audit procedure that allows for such differentiation —a testing procedure that reveals the individual's health status so that the disabled can be identified. To some extent, the situation without such an audit looks very much like what is observed in a number of countries where a clear abuse of disability insurance programs results in a low participation rate of elderly workers. The situation with the audit looks more like the one that prevails at the start of social security programs. In fact, a number of economists now advocate increasing the age of retirement by eliminating disability insurance as an early retirement program.

We have already cited the literature that shows disability insurance and other programs as standard routes for exiting the labor force before the normal retirement age. In addition, some studies deal specifically with disability insurance. In the United States, work has been done on the interactions between disability insurance and the labor market. Parsons (1980), in a widely quoted paper, shows that the social security program explains a large fraction of the postwar decline in prime-age labor-force participation. This study was followed by several that never disputed the disincentive effects of disability insurance but questioned its magnitude (see, e.g., Bound, 1989; Parsons, 1991). This literature reveals one issue that concerns the number of truly disabled workers and another issue that concerns the number of beneficiaries of disability insurance. Putting aside employment policy considerations, these two numbers reveal the difficulties that are encountered when trying to identify truly disabled workers in a world of asymmetric information.

## 7.2  A Simple Model of Disability Insurance

### 7.2.1  Preferences and Types of Individuals

The setting is inspired by Cremer, Lozachmeur, and Pestieau (2004b). Consider an individual with productivity $w$, and divide his lifetime (with duration normalized to one) into a period of full activity and a period of retirement. Assume away any liquidity constraint and posit a zero rate of interest and a time discount rate. The budget constraint is then given by

$$\int_0^1 c(t)\,dt = \int_0^z w\,dt,$$

where $c(t)$ is instantaneous consumption and $z$ ($z \le 1$) is the age of retirement. Lifetime utility is defined as

$$U = \int_0^1 u(c(t))\,dt - \int_0^z r(t)\,dt,$$

where $u(\cdot)$ is a strictly concave instantaneous utility function and $r(t)$ denotes an increasing function of effort disutility. As shown below, $r(t)$ can be viewed as a mixture of a taste for retirement leisure and a physical and mental inability to work additional years. We assume that $r(t)$ varies across individuals and increases over a lifetime. Under these assumptions, the utility function and the budget constraint can be rewritten as

$$U = u(c) - \varphi(z)$$

and

$hc = wz,$

where

$$\varphi(z) = \int_0^z r(t)\, dt. \tag{7.1}$$

In other words, there is a perfect smoothing out of consumption over time. We use this reduced form for utility and budget constraints throughout the chapter.

Three types of individuals are indexed: $i = H, L, D$. We assume[2]

$$r_H(t) < r_L(t) = r_D(t) \text{ for every } t, \tag{7.2}$$

which from (7.1) also implies $\varphi_H(z) < \varphi_L(z) = \varphi_D(z)$. Individuals of type $H$ are hard-working or healthy; they have a low disutility of labor. Type $D$ (disabled) and $L$ (leisure-prone or lazy) have the same (high) disutility of labor, which is higher than that for type $H$. They thus have the same preferences for consumption and leisure. However, they differ in their health status. Specifically, we think of type $D$ as truly disabled, so that the high disutility of labor is due to poor health. Individuals of type $L$, on the other hand, are in good health but are leisure-prone. One may thus think of health status as a second dimension of heterogeneity. This heterogeneity is not reflected in the individual's preferences for consumption and length of activity. However, it determines the preferences of the social planner, who will want to help the disabled but not the leisure-prone individuals (see below for further discussion).

Observe that (7.2) can also be written as

$$\frac{\varphi_H'(z)}{u'(c)} < \frac{\varphi_L'(z)}{u'(c)} = \frac{\varphi_D'(z)}{u'(c)}, \quad z \in [0,1],\ c > 0, \tag{7.3}$$

which can be interpreted as a single-crossing property. For any bundle in the $(z,c)$ space, $L$ and $D$ type individuals have steeper indifference curves than $H$ type individuals.

### 7.2.2  Policy

We now introduce the possibility of a disability or retirement insurance scheme that consists of a payroll tax $\tau$ and a (pension) benefit function $p(z)$ and that depends on the retirement age. This tax-transfer scheme $(\tau, p(z))$ encompasses disability and retirement insurance programs. For simplicity, we often refer to this as *social insurance*. It can be represented by a nonlinear tax function

$$T(z) \equiv \int_0^z w\tau \, dt - \int_z^1 p(z) \, dt$$

$$= z\tau w - (1-z)p(z).$$

Differentiating $T(z)$ with respect to $z$ yields the marginal tax on postponed work that underlies the retirement insurance program

$$T'(z) = \tau w + p(z) - (1-z)p'(z).$$

This expression shows the cost of delaying retirement, which is given by $\tau w$, the payroll tax plus $p(z)$, the forgone pension minus the increase in benefit $(p'(z))$, if any, over the length of retirement $(1-z)$. We refer to a social insurance program as *actuarially neutral* at the margin if $T'(z) = 0$.[3]

For future reference, note that a consumer's problem under a nonlinear function $T(z)$ can be written as

$$\max_z \ u(wz - T(z)) - \varphi(z). \tag{7.4}$$

From the first-order condition, we then obtain

$$\frac{\varphi'(z)}{u'(c)} = w - T'(z). \tag{7.5}$$

In other words, a nonzero marginal tax implies a wedge between (1) the marginal rate of substitution between work and consumption and (2) the marginal productivity of labor. This relationship is important for the interpretation of our results below.

## 7.3   Different Social Weights

Let us now return to the interpretation of $\varphi(z)$—that is, to the disutility for prolonged activity. This disutility is affected both by taste and by health factors. Some people want to retire early because they have a strong preference for leisure and a desire to enjoy a long retirement period. Other people want to retire because physically they cannot work any longer. To account for this apparent ambiguity, we distinguish disabled ($D$) and leisure-prone individuals ($L$). If disability were easily observable, there would be no problem, but in some cases it is observable only at a cost—the cost of medical tests.

Recall that $D$ and $L$ have the same function $\varphi_i(z)$; in other words, $\varphi_L(z) = \varphi_D(z)$. However, the social planner is not ready to consider those two types as identical. We assume that the social planner wants to help the disabled workers but not the leisure-prone ones. More precisely, the high disutility for prolonged activity is considered to be "legitimate" (and fully accounted for in welfare) for the disabled but not for the lazy individuals. One way of introducing such a distinction is to assume a weighted social-welfare function with lower weights on type $L$ than on type $D$. This leaves open the issue of which weight to attach to $H$. To keep things simple, we introduce welfare weights $\psi_i$ $(i = H, L, D)$ such that $\psi_L < \psi_D = \psi_H$. An alternative approach with paternalistic rather than Paretian social preferences is considered in section 7.4, where the disutility for the lazy type $L$ is evaluated with $\varphi_H$ rather than $\varphi_L$.

### 7.3.1   Full-Information Optimum and Laissez-Faire

The first-best problem is given by

$$\max_{c_i, z_i} \sum_i \psi_i \pi_i [u(c_i) - \varphi_i(z_i)] + \mu \sum_i \pi_i (w z_i - c_i). \tag{7.6}$$

This gives the efficiency conditions

$$\frac{\varphi_H'(z_H)}{u'(c_H)} = \frac{\varphi_L'(z_L)}{u'(c_L)} = \frac{\varphi_L'(z_D)}{u'(c_D)} = w, \tag{7.7}$$

which, not surprisingly, are equivalent to (7.5) with $T'(z) = 0$. With objective (7.6), the social optimum is Pareto efficient, and we have the usual first-best tradeoffs.

We also have

$$\psi_H u'(c_H) = \psi_L u'(c_L) = \psi_D u'(c_D) = \mu, \tag{7.8}$$

so that consumption levels and retirement ages are ranked as follows:

$$c_D = c_H > c_L$$

$$z_D < z_H \quad z_D < z_L \quad z_H \gtrless z_L.$$

With this specification, type $D$ individuals end up retiring earlier than the two other ones. They consume as much as $H$ and more than $L$. In other words, they are compensated for their disability not only by retiring earlier but also by receiving higher benefits (which is questionable).

The laissez-faire solution does not depend on the social objective. Consequently, it is given by equation (7.7) with the implication that $c_D = c_L < c_H$ and $z_D = z_L < z_H$. Observe that to decentralize the full-information solution, one simply needs lump-sum transfers from $H$ and $L$ to $D$ and between $H$ and $L$ (the direction depending on the weights). The retirement choice does not have to be distorted. This is because the weighted objective function necessarily yields a Pareto-efficient solution, so that the second welfare theorem applies.

### 7.3.2 Unobservable Types: A Second-Best Solution

Let us now turn to the second-best problem, where types are not observable. With three types, we then have to add six incentive compatibility constraints.[4] In particular, we have

$$u(c_L) - \varphi_L(z_L) \geq u(c_D) - \varphi_L(z_D) \tag{7.9}$$

for type $L$ and

$$u(c_D) - \varphi_D(z_D) \geq u(c_L) - \varphi_L(z_L) \tag{7.10}$$

for type $D$. Recalling that $\varphi_L(z) \equiv \varphi_D(z)$ and combining (7.10) and (7.9) yields, not surprisingly,

$$u(c_L) - \varphi_L(z_L) = u(c_D) - \varphi_L(z_D). \tag{7.11}$$

In other words, because $D$ and $L$ have the same preferences over $c$ and $z$, their utility levels must be equalized at any incentive-compatible allocation. The simplest way to achieve (7.11) is, to offer the same consumption bundle to the two types $c_L = c_D$, and consequently $z_L = z_D$. As becomes clear below, this is effectively optimal even when it is not a priori imposed.[5]

When types $D$ and $L$ are pooled, the problem of the social planner is

$$\max \sum_i \psi_i \pi_i [u(c_i) - \varphi_i(z_i)] + \mu \sum_i \pi_i (w z_i - c_i)$$

$$+ \lambda [u(c_H) - \varphi_H(z_H) - u(c_L) + \varphi_H(z_L)],$$

where we use the subscript $L$ for both $L$ and $D$'s choices of $z$ and $c$. The first-order conditions with respect to $z_H$ and $c_H$ yield the traditional no distortion at the top: the marginal rate of substitution of type $H$ continues to be given by (7.7). The first-order conditions with respect to $z_L = z_D$ and $c_L = c_D$ are

$$\frac{\varphi'_L(z_L)}{u'(c_L)} = w - \frac{\lambda}{(\psi_L \pi_L + \psi_D \pi_D - \lambda)} \frac{[\varphi'_L(z_L) - \varphi'_H(z_L)]}{u'(c_L)}, \qquad (7.12)$$

where $(\psi_L \pi_L + \psi_D \pi_D - \lambda) > 0$ follows from the first-order condition with respect to $c_L = c_D$, while the single-crossing property (7.3) implies $\varphi'_L(z_L) > \varphi'_H(z_H)$. Consequently, we have a downward distortion and a positive marginal tax on $z_L = z_D$. We have a rather standard optimal tax problem. A distortion on $z$ is here justified only by incentive arguments. According to our assumptions on preferences, a downward distortion is called for to relax an otherwise binding self-selection constraint.

### 7.3.3   A Second-Best Solution with Auditing

The lack of observability of health status can be costly in terms of welfare. To improve on this second-best solution, ways need to be found to distinguish types $L$ and $D$. A traditional way to achieve this is to use disability evaluations.[6]

To study the implications of such a policy, we adopt a very simple form of audit that perfectly reveals an individual's "health status."[7] More precisely, the audit indicates whether an individual is of type $D$ and can be used to distinguish between $D$ and $L$ individuals. Observe that the audit also reveals mimicking between $H$ and $D$ but *not* between $H$ and $L$ (who are both in good health). When a fraction $\sigma$ of type $D$'s reports are subject to testing, the corresponding audit cost is given by $k(\pi_D \sigma)$. Thus, an individual who is caught cheating is subject to a sanction that reduces his utility to some exogenous and "low" utility level of $\underline{u}$. With this assumption, we have to modify the revenue constraints of the government and then consider six incentive compatibility relations. We have

$$\sum_i \pi_i(wz_i - c_i) - \sigma(\pi_D k) = 0.$$

Here are the new constraints:

$(LD)$: $u(c_L) - \varphi_L(z_L) - (1 - \sigma)(u(c_D) - \varphi_L(z_D)) - \sigma \underline{u} \geq 0$

$(DL)$: $u(c_D) - \varphi_L(z_D) - u(c_L) + \varphi_L(z_L) \geq 0$

$(HD)$: $u(c_H) - \varphi_H(z_H) - (1 - \pi)(u(c_D) - \varphi_H(z_D)) - \sigma\underline{u} \geq 0$

$(DH)$: $u(c_D) - \varphi_L(z_D) - u(c_H) + \varphi_L(z_H) \geq 0$

$(HL)$: $u(c_H) - \varphi_H(z_H) - u(c_L) + \varphi_H(z_L) \geq 0$

$(LH)$: $u(c_L) - \varphi_L(z_L) - u(c_H) + \varphi_L(z_H) \geq 0$.

The properties of the solution depend on which of the incentive constraints are binding at the optimum. With six incentives, the number of potential combinations of binding incentive constraint is quite large. To reduce the number of cases, we first make some plausible assumptions. First, we assume that the weights are such that the "upward" constraints $(DH)$ and $(LH)$ are not binding. With $\psi_D = \psi_H > \psi_L$, it is clear that $(LH)$ can potentially be binding when the weight on $L$ becomes very small. We assume that this is not the case. Second, we restrict our attention to settings where $(LD)$ is binding. This, in turn, immediately implies that $(DL)$ is not binding (as long as $\sigma > 0$).

The Lagrangian expression that is associated with the problem of the social planner is then given by

$$\mathcal{L} = \sum_i \psi_i \pi_i [u(c_i) - \varphi_i(z_i)] + \mu \left[ \sum_i \pi_i (wz_i - c_i) - k(\pi_D \sigma) \right]$$

$$+ \lambda_{LD}[u(c_L) - \varphi_L(z_L) - (1 - \sigma)(u(c_D) - \varphi_L(z_D)) - \sigma\underline{u}]$$

$$+ \lambda_{HL}[u(c_H) - \varphi_H(z_H) - u(c_L) + \varphi_H(z_L)]$$

$$+ \lambda_{HD}[u(c_H) - \varphi_H(z_H) - (1 - \sigma)(u(c_D) - \varphi_H(z_D)) - \sigma\underline{u}].$$

We have seven first-order conditions:

$$\frac{\partial \mathcal{L}}{\partial c_H} = \psi_H \pi_H u'(c_H) - \pi_H \mu + (\lambda_{HL} + \lambda_{HD})u'(c_H) = 0$$

$$\frac{\partial \mathcal{L}}{\partial z_H} = -\psi_H \pi_H \varphi_H'(z_H) + \pi_H \mu w - (\lambda_{HL} + \lambda_{HD})\varphi_H'(z_H) = 0$$

$$\frac{\partial \mathcal{L}}{\partial c_L} = \psi_L \pi_L u'(c_L) - \pi_L \mu + (\lambda_{LD} - \lambda_{HL})u'(c_L) = 0$$

$$\frac{\partial \mathcal{L}}{\partial z_L} = -\psi_L \pi_L \varphi_L'(z_L) + \pi_L \mu w - \lambda_{LD}\varphi_L'(z_L) + \lambda_{HL}\varphi_H'(z_L) = 0$$

$$\frac{\partial \mathcal{L}}{\partial c_D} = \psi_D \pi_D u'(c_D) - \pi_D \mu - (\lambda_{LD} + \lambda_{HD})(1 - \sigma)u'(c_D) = 0$$

$$\frac{\partial \mathcal{L}}{\partial z_D} = -\varphi_D \pi_D \varphi_L'(z_D) + \pi_D \mu w + \lambda_{LD}(1 - \sigma)\varphi_L'(z_D)$$

$$+ \lambda_{HD}(1 - \sigma)\varphi_H'(z_D) = 0$$

$$\frac{\partial \mathcal{L}}{\partial \pi} = -\mu \pi_D k' + \lambda_{LD}[u(c_D) - \varphi_L(z_D) - \underline{u}]$$

$$+ \lambda_{HD}[u(c_D) - \varphi_H(z_D) - \underline{u}] \leq 0.$$

The first six conditions can be rearranged as follows:[8]

$$MRS_H = \frac{\varphi_H'(z_H)}{u'(c_H)} = w \tag{7.13}$$

$$MRS_L = \frac{\varphi_L'(z_L)}{u'(c_L)} = w - \frac{\lambda_{HL}[\varphi_L'(z_L) - \varphi_H'(z_L)]}{(\psi_L \pi_L + \lambda_{LD} - \lambda_{HL})u'(c_L)} \leq w \tag{7.14}$$

$$MRS_D = \frac{\varphi_D'(z_D)}{u'(c_D)} = w - \frac{\lambda_{HD}(1 - \sigma)[\varphi_L'(z_D) - \varphi_H'(z_D)]}{\psi_D \pi_D - (\lambda_{LD} + \lambda_{HD})(1 - \sigma)u'(c_D)} \leq w. \tag{7.15}$$

In Cremer, Lozachmeur, and Pestieau (2004c), we use these first-order conditions to derive the following lemma, which further reduces the number of regimes to be considered.

LEMMA 7.1   A solution with $\lambda_{HD} > 0$ and $\lambda_{HL} = 0$ is not possible.

Lemma 1 and the assumption made above imply that we are left with the following three regimes:

| Regime | Binding Incentive Constraints |
| --- | --- |
| 1 | $(HL), (HD), (LD)$ |
| 2 | $(HL), (LD)$ |
| 3 | $(LD)$ |

The numerical illustrations provided in the next section show that each of these three regimes can occur. From the first-order conditions, we then obtain the following results for the different types of individuals:

• **Type $H$**  Whatever the regime, we know from (7.13) that the *marginal* tax on $z$ is zero for the type $H$ individual. This is the usual no-distortion-at-the-top result obtained because no incentive constraint toward these individuals is binding.

• **Type $L$**  We know from (7.14) that this individual is subject to a downward distortion on his or her choice of retirement if (and only if) $\lambda_{HL} > 0$—that is, in regimes 1 and 2.

• **Type $D$**  Using (7.15), we see that there may or may not be a distortion in the choice of $z$ for this type, depending on $\lambda_{HD}$. When $\lambda_{HD} > 0$, $z_D$ is subject to a downward distortion, which does not come as a surprise. This occurs in regime 1 only. In the two other regimes, $\lambda_{HD} = 0$ and individuals of type $D$ are subject to no distortion. This may appear surprising at first because an incentive constraint toward $D$—namely, $(LD)$—is binding. However, since $D$ and $L$ have the same indifference curves, a distortion would not be an effective way to relax this incentive constraint.[9]

An interesting question is whether the introduction of an audit makes the lazy retire later than the disabled. The answer depends on the regime. In regime 3, neither type $D$ nor type $L$ is subject to distortions. Since type $D$ workers are on a higher indifference curve, we unambiguously have $z_L > z_D$. In regime 2, there is an implicit tax on $z_L$, but the disabled receive a higher transfer than the lazy. These transfers have an effect that fosters early retirement, so that the comparison between $z_L$ and $z_D$ is ambiguous. In regime 1, where the comparison between $z_D$ and $z_L$ seems ambiguous (both being distorted downward), we can rank them unambiguously. To see this, we write $(HL)$, $(LD)$, and $(HD)$ as equalities and combine them, yielding

$$\varphi_L(z_L) - \varphi_H(z_L) = (1 - \sigma)[\varphi_L(z_D) - \varphi_H(z_D)].$$

By convexity of $\varphi(\cdot)$, this entails $z_D > z_L$. Consequently, in regime 1 we do have the result that disabled individuals retire later than lazy individuals.

All these results are valid for any level of the audit probability $(0 < \sigma < 1)$. To determine the *optimal* level of $\sigma$, we have to use the first-order condition (7.12). It shows that the determination of $\sigma$ involves a tradeoff between costs $(\mu \pi_D k')$ and benefits that depends on the utility gap between truth telling and being caught. Evidently, the larger the audit costs, and the larger $\underline{u}$, the lower will be $\sigma$. Conversely, the lower the audit costs, the higher the $\pi$. Note, however, that auditing with probability one ($\sigma = 1$) is never optimal. This is a standard result in auditing models. It directly follows from (7.12) by observing that when $\sigma = 1$, (LD) and (HD) are satisfied with strict inequality. Consequently, we would have $\lambda_{LD} = \lambda_{HD} = 0$, which implies that the derivative is negative. This makes sense because when incentive constraints are satisfied with strict inequality, they continue to be satisfied when audit probability (and hence audit cost) is slightly reduced.

Not much can be said analytically about the factors explaining the occurrence of one regime as opposed than another. However, it is clear that $\sigma$ (which, in turn, is determined by audit costs) will play a crucial role. In particular, when $\sigma$ is high enough, regime 1 cannot occur. To see this, suppose that (LD) and (HL) bind. Using these expressions for the incentive constraints, it then follows that (HD) is not binding when

$$\varphi_L(z_L) - \varphi_H(z_L) - (1 - \sigma)[\varphi_L(z_D) - \varphi_H(z_D)] > 0. \tag{7.16}$$

This necessarily holds when $\sigma$ is close to one.

Figure 7.1 illustrates the above solution for regime 2, as well as the solution without audit studied in section 7.3.2.[10] Without an audit, individuals of type $H$ consume bundle $h$, and individuals $D$ and $L$ who cannot be distinguished consume $l = d$. With an audit, we have $l$ and $d$ for the lazy and the disabled, respectively. Now the disabled

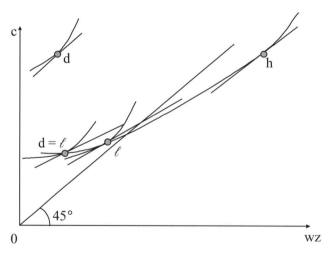

**Figure 7.1**
Paretian objective: Solution without and with auditing

could get a consumption level as high as that of the individuals $h$. With $\lambda_{HD} = 0$ (regime 2), they do not face any distortion.[11] They work less if the income effect is sufficiently effective. Individuals $L$ work more and consume more than in the pooling equilibrium. We now turn to a numerical illustration.

### 7.3.4  Illustration

$$u(c_i, z_i) = \ln c_i - \alpha_i \frac{z_i^{1/2}}{2},$$

with the following parameter values:

|            | H    | L    | D    |
|------------|------|------|------|
| $\alpha_i$ | 1    | 5    | 5    |
| $\pi_i$    | 0.6  | 0.1  | 0.3  |
| $\psi_i$   | 1    | 0.3  | 1    |
| $w_i$      | 100  | 100  | 100  |

We consider three audit technologies depending on their cost. Audit 1 is relatively expensive ($k(\pi) = 2000\pi^2$) and implies $\sigma = 0.06$, $\lambda_{HL} > 0$, $\lambda_{LD} > 0$, and $\lambda_{HD} > 0$ (regime 1). Audit 2 is cheaper ($k(\pi) = 1000\pi^2$) and implies $\sigma = 0.10$ with $\lambda_{HL} > 0$ and $\lambda_{LD} > 0$ (regime 2). Finally, audit 3 is the cheapest ($k(\pi) = 100\pi^2$) and implies $\sigma = 0.49$ (regime 3). In all cases, $\underline{u} = 0$. The results are given in table 7.1.

First, observe that starting from the no-auditing-pooling solution, introducing audit 1 leads to regime 1, where all three incentive-compatibility constraints are binding. Turning to a less expensive technology (and thus to a higher level of audit) implies a regime where ($HD$) no longer binds. For even smaller audit costs, we obtain regime 3. If the audit technology were to be completely costless, however, we would have either only ($HL$) binding if $\psi_L$ is relatively high or the first-best solution if $\psi_L$ is relatively low.[12]

Second, we observe that in all the second-best solutions the consumption of $D$ is kept below that of $H$, whereas in the first-best solutions the two types have the same consumption. Not surprisingly, the difference between $c_H$ and $c_D$ decreases as the audit probability increases. Furthermore, in the pooling solution we have $c_D = c_L$, while with auditing $c_D > c_L$ holds. As expected, the difference between $c_D$

**Table 7.1**
Numerical example: Paretian objective

| Types | First-Best | | | Pooling | | |
|---|---|---|---|---|---|---|
| | $D$ | $L$ | $H$ | $D$ | $L$ | $H$ |
| $c$ | 88.39 | 26.51 | 88.39 | 54 | 54 | 92.48 |
| $z$ | 0.22 | 0.75 | 1.13 | 0.30 | 0.30 | 1.08 |
| $u$ | 4.35 | 1.85 | 3.84 | 3.75 | 3.75 | 3.94 |
| $T'(z)$ | 0 | 0 | 0 | 0.17 | 0.17 | 0 |

| Types | Audit 1 | | | Audit 2 | | | Audit 3 | | |
|---|---|---|---|---|---|---|---|---|---|
| | $D$ | $L$ | $H$ | $D$ | $L$ | $H$ | $D$ | $L$ | $H$ |
| $c$ | 65.29 | 49.72 | 89.32 | 70.74 | 48.23 | 87.94 | 81.42 | 46.59 | 84.95 |
| $z$ | 0.29 | 0.28 | 1.11 | 0.28 | 0.30 | 1.13 | 0.24 | 0.43 | 1.17 |
| $u$ | 3.95 | 3.70 | 3.86 | 4.05 | 3.64 | 3.83 | 4.24 | 3.38 | 3.74 |
| $T'(z)$ | 0.03 | 0.28 | 0 | 0 | 0.26 | 0 | 0 | 0 | 0 |

and $c_L$ increases as audits become cheaper and more intense and thus allow for better screening. Finally, in regime 1 $D$ retires later than $L$, which is in line with the analytical result obtained above. In the other two regimes, however, we have $z_D < z_L$, even though $L$ faces a positive marginal tax in regime 2 while $D$'s marginal tax is zero. This illustrates the idea that the income effects (transfer to $D$) can dominate the substitution effects (marginal distortions).

## 7.4   An Alternative Specification

We now consider an alternative specification in which the social planner paternalistically attributes to the lazy workers a disutility $R_L$ rather than $R_H$. In other words, he wants them to work more and not to consume less. As above, we start by considering the full-information solution.

### 7.4.1   A Full-Information Solution and Decentralization

With the paternalistic approach, the full-information problem is given by

$$\max \sum_i \pi_i u(c_i) - \pi_H \varphi_H(z_H) - \pi_L \varphi_H(z_L) - \pi_D \varphi_L(z_D) + \mu \sum_i \pi_i(c_i - wz_i).$$

The solution is easily obtained. Both healthy types (namely, $H$ and $L$) are assigned the same retirement age. The disabled individuals retire earlier, and all individuals have the same consumption level:

$$z_D < z_L = z_H \quad \text{and} \quad c_D = c_L = c_D.$$

The laissez-faire solution does not depend on the social objective and is thus the same as in section 7.3. Consequently, it is given by equation (7.10) with the implication that $c_D = c_L < c_H$ and $z_D = z_L < z_H$. Decentralizing the first-best solution, however, is now not as simple as in the nonpaternalistic specification. Lump-sum transfers are not sufficient; a subsidy (negative marginal tax) on the labor supply of type $L$ individuals is also needed. To see this, note that the decentralized choice of $z_L$ is determined by

$$(w - T'(z_L))u'(c_L) - \varphi_L'(z_L) = 0, \tag{7.17}$$

which coincides with the socially optimal one

$$wu'(c_L) - \varphi_H'(z_L) = 0 \tag{7.18}$$

when the marginal tax rate is given by

$$T'(z_L) = -\frac{[\varphi_L'(z_L) - \varphi_H'(z_L)]}{u'(c_L)} < 0, \tag{7.19}$$

so that we effectively have a subsidy. In other words, the rate of subsidy is equal to the difference between "private" and the "social" marginal valuation for $z_L$ (evaluated at the optimal allocation). Paternalism introduces a wedge between private and social valuations of type $L$'s labor supply, and the decentralization of the optimum requires a Pigouvian subsidy.

### 7.4.2 Unobservable Types: A Second-Best Solution

Let us now turn to the second-best problem, where types are not observable. With three types, we have to add six incentive constraints. As in section 7.3.2, we start with the no-audit case showing that only $(HL)$, $(HD)$, and $(LD)$ can be binding. When $(HD)$ is binding together with $(HL)$ and $(LD)$, one has a pooling optimum. The program is now

$$\max \sum \pi_i u(c_i) - \pi_H \varphi_H(z_H) - \pi_L \varphi_H(z_L) - \pi_D \varphi_L(z_L)$$

$$+ \mu \sum \pi_i(w z_i - c_i) + \lambda_{HL}[u(c_H) - \varphi_H(z_H) - u(c_L) + \varphi_H(z_L)]$$

$$+ \lambda_{HD}[u(c_H) - \varphi_H(z_H) - u(c_D) + \varphi_H(z_D)]$$

$$+ \lambda_{LD}[u(c_L) - \varphi_L(z_L) - u(c_D) + \varphi_L(z_D)].$$

The first-order conditions with respect to $z_H$ and $c_H$ yield the traditional no-distortion-at-the-top result: the marginal rate of substitution of type $H$ continues to be given by (7.7). The first-order conditions with respect to $z_L$, $z_D$, $c_L$, and $c_D$ are

$$(\pi_L - \lambda_{HL} + \lambda_{LD})u'(c_L) + \mu\pi_L = 0 \tag{7.20}$$

$$(\pi_D - \lambda_{HD} - \lambda_{LD})u'(c_D) + \mu\pi_D = 0 \tag{7.21}$$

$$-\pi_L \varphi_H'(z_L) - \mu\pi_L w + \lambda_{HL}\varphi_H'(z_L) - \lambda_{LD}\varphi_L'(z_L) = 0 \tag{7.22}$$

$$-\pi_D \varphi_L'(z_D) - \mu\pi_D w + \lambda_{HD}\varphi_H'(z_D) + \lambda_{LD}\varphi_L'(z_D) = 0. \tag{7.23}$$

This yields

$$MRS_L = \frac{\varphi_L'(z_L)}{u'(c_L)} = w + \left[\frac{\pi_L - \lambda_{HL}}{\pi_L - \lambda_{HL} + \lambda_{LD}}\right]\left[\frac{\varphi_L'(z_L) - \varphi_H'(z_L)}{u'(c_L)}\right], \tag{7.24}$$

where $\pi_L - \lambda_{HL} + \lambda_{LD} > 0$ from (7.20), while the sign of $(\pi_L - \lambda)$ appears to be ambiguous. Furthermore, we have

$$MRS_D = \frac{\varphi_D'(z_D)}{u'(c_D)} = w - \frac{\lambda_{HD}}{(\pi_D - \lambda_{LD} - \lambda_{HD})}\left[\frac{\varphi_L'(z_D) - \varphi_H'(z_D)}{u'(c_D)}\right], \tag{7.25}$$

where $(\pi_D - \lambda_{LD} - \lambda_{HD}) > 0$ from (7.21) so that we necessarily have a downward distortion for type $D$'s choice of $z$. The new feature is that $D$ and $L$ are no longer necessarily pooled even when there is no audit. More precisely, we have the following lemma:

LEMMA 7.2 The optimum pools $D$ and $L$, if and only if $\varphi_L'(z_L)/u'(c_L) < w$—that is, iff $\pi_L < \lambda_{HL}$.

To interpret this result, consider equation (7.24). The distortion on $z_L$ is of ambiguous sign. When $\pi_L > \lambda_{HL}$, the right side of (7.24) is larger than $w$ so that we have an upward distortion on labor supply (a negative marginal tax rate). Conversely, $\pi_L < \lambda_{HL}$ yields a downward distortion and thus a positive marginal tax. To understand the role played by this term, note that the distortion in type $L$'s labor supply is determined by balancing two conflicting objectives. First, there is the standard (Mirrlees-type) incentive effect, which calls for a downward distortion (positive marginal tax) on $L$'s labor supply to relax the incentive constraint from type $H$ to type $L$. The significance of this effect depends on $\lambda_{HL}$, the Lagrange multiplier of this incentive constraint. Second, there is a "paternalistic" effect, which calls for an increase in type $L$'s labor supply compared to the laissez-faire level. Recall that the social disutility of $L$'s labor is smaller than his private disutility. This pleads in favor of an upward distortion (a negative marginal tax). This effect is more significant as the proportion of group $L$ in the economy is larger. When $\pi_L$ is large enough, the paternalistic consideration is dominant, so that there is a marginal subsidy on $z_L$. In this case, there is no reason to pool individuals $L$ and $D$ because there is no need for distortion on $z_D$.

However, when $\pi_L$ is small, incentive considerations dominate, and a marginal tax is called for on $z_L$. In this case, individuals $L$ and $D$ are necessarily pooled to prevent individuals $H$ from mimicking individuals $D$.

To sum up, when $\pi_L$ is large enough, the optimum entails separation between type $D$ and type $L$ individuals. In this case, there is no distortion on $z_D$ and a marginal subsidy on $z_L$. When $\pi_L$ is small, one has a pooling optimum with a marginal tax on $z_L$ and $z_D$. Note, finally, that in the separating optimum, one necessarily always has $z_L > z_D$.

### 7.4.3   A Second-Best Solution with Auditing in the Paternalistic Case

Introducing an audit, as in section 7.3.3, while continuing to assume that the upward constraints $(LH)$ and $(DH)$ are not binding, the social-planner problem can now be written as the maximization of

$$\mathcal{L}_2 = \sum_{i=1}^{3} \pi_i u(c_i) - \pi_H \varphi_H(z_H) - \pi_L \varphi_H(z_L) - \pi_D \varphi_L(z_D)$$

$$+ \mu \left[ \sum_{i=1}^{3} \pi_i (w z_i - c_i) - \pi_D k \sigma \right]$$

$$+ \lambda_{LD}[u(c_L) - \varphi_L(z_L) - (1 - \sigma)(u(c_D) - \varphi_L(z_D)) - \sigma \underline{u}]$$

$$+ \lambda_{HL}[u(c_H) - \varphi_H(z_H) - u(c_L) + \varphi_H(z_L)]$$

$$+ \lambda_{HD}[u(c_H) - \varphi_H(z_H) - (1 - \sigma)(u(c_D) - \varphi_H(z_D)) - \sigma\underline{u}]$$

$$+ \lambda_{DL}[u(c_D) - \varphi_D(z_D) - u(c_L) + \varphi_D(z_L)].$$

The first-order conditions are given by

$$\frac{\partial \mathcal{L}_2}{\partial c_H} = \pi_H u'(c_H) - \pi_H \mu + (\lambda_{HL} + \lambda_{HD})u'(c_H) = 0,$$

$$\frac{\partial \mathcal{L}_2}{\partial z_H} = -\pi_H \varphi_H'(z_H) + \pi_H \mu w - (\lambda_{HL} + \lambda_{HD})\varphi_H'(z_H) = 0,$$

$$\frac{\partial \mathcal{L}_2}{\partial c_L} = \pi_L u'(c_L) - \pi_L \mu + (\lambda_{LD} - \lambda_{HL} - \lambda_{DL})u'(c_L) = 0,$$

$$\frac{\partial \mathcal{L}_2}{\partial z_L} = -\pi_L \varphi_H'(z_L) + \pi_L \mu w - (\lambda_{LD} - \lambda_{DL})\varphi_L'(z_L) + \lambda_{HL}\varphi_H'(z_L) = 0,$$

$$\frac{\partial \mathcal{L}_2}{\partial c_D} = \pi_D u'(c_D) - \pi_D \mu + \lambda_{DL}u'(c_D) - (\lambda_{LD} + \lambda_{HD})(1 - \pi)u'(c_D) = 0,$$

$$\frac{\partial \mathcal{L}_2}{\partial z_D} = -\pi_D \varphi_L'(z_D) + \pi_D \mu w - \lambda_{DL}\varphi_L'(z_D)$$

$$+ (\lambda_{LD}\varphi_L'(z_D) + \lambda_{HD}\varphi_H'(z_D))(1 - \pi) = 0,$$

$$\frac{\partial \mathcal{L}_2}{\partial \pi} = -\mu \pi_D k + \lambda_{LD}(u(c_D) - \varphi_L(z_D) - \underline{u})$$

$$+ \lambda_{HD}(u(c_D) - \varphi_H(z_D) - \underline{u}) \leq 0. \tag{7.26}$$

Combining and rearranging these conditions yield the following expressions for the marginal rates of substitution of the different types:

$$\frac{\varphi_H'(z_H)}{u'(c_H)} = w. \tag{7.27}$$

$$\frac{\varphi_L'(z_L)}{u'(c_L)} = w + \frac{(\pi_L - \lambda_{HL})[\varphi_L'(z_L) - \varphi_H'(z_L)]}{(\pi_L + \lambda_{LD} - \lambda_{DL} - \lambda_{HL})u'(c_L)} \lesseqqgtr w \tag{7.28}$$

$$\frac{\varphi_L'(z_D)}{u'(c_D)} = w - \frac{\lambda_{HD}(1 - \pi)[\varphi_L'(z_D) - \varphi_H'(z_D)]}{(\pi_D - (\lambda_{LD} + \lambda_{HD})(1 - \pi) + \lambda_{DL})u'(c_D)} \leq w. \tag{7.29}$$

Before commenting on these expressions, it is necessary to determine the possible regimes. To reduce the number of cases, we can first show that lemma 7.1 continues to hold in the alternative specification. Next, in Cremer, Lozachmeur, and Pestieau (2003), we provide a sequence of additional lemmas that show that in the paternalistic case only two regimes are possible, given by the following:

| Regime | Binding-Incentive Constraints |
| --- | --- |
| 1 | $(HL), (HD), (LD)$ |
| 2 | $(HL), (LD)$ |

Consequently, it turns out that regime 3, where only $(LD)$ was binding, cannot arise here.

Let us now turn to the interpretation of conditions (7.27) through (7.29), while taking into account that in both possible regimes $(DL)$ is not binding, so that we have $\lambda_{DL} = 0$. Equation (7.27) is the usual no-distortion-at-the-top property. Turning to (7.28), we observe that $(\pi_L + \lambda_{LD} - \lambda_{HL}) > 0$, while the sign of $(\pi_L - \lambda_{HL})$ is ambiguous. As in the preceding section, when $\pi_L > \lambda_{HL}$, paternalistic considerations are dominant, leading to a marginal subsidy on $z_L$. When $\pi_L < \lambda_{HL}$, incentive considerations dominate, and a positive marginal tax on $z_L$ is optimal.

On the other hand, for the interpretation of (7.29), we have to distinguish regime 2 with $\lambda_{HD} = 0$ from regime 1 with $\lambda_{HD} > 0$. The results are exactly like those that occur with the first specification. In regime 2, $\lambda_{HD} = 0$, there is no distortion in the choice of retirement for the truly disabled. The mimicking individual $L$ has the same indifference curves as individual $D$. Consequently, there is no way to create a distortion that hurts the mimicker more than the mimicked. Put differently, a distortion is not an effective way to relax the incentive constraint. Consequently, the retirement choice of type $D$ is treated *at the margin* exactly like that of the type $H$ individual (zero marginal tax). By contrast, in regime 1 we have $\lambda_{HL} > 0$, and there is a distortion toward earlier retirement. This distortion relaxes the incentive constraint $(HD)$ but has no effect on $(LD)$. As in section 7.3.4, this distortion is likely to be effective for a relatively low probability of auditing.

The comparison between $z_L$ and $z_D$ is the same as above. However, note that regime 1 cannot occur when there is a marginal subsidy on $z_L$. To see this, recall that regime 1 implies a distortion on $z_D$ and $z_L < z_D$. Since $D$ is on a higher indifference curve, this is incompatible with a marginal subsidy on $z_L$. We summarize this in the following lemma:

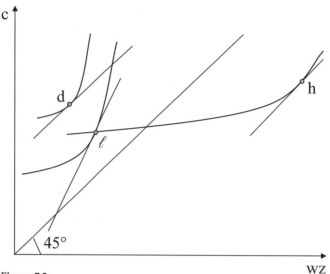

**Figure 7.2**
Paternalistic objective: Solution with auditing

LEMMA 7.3   When $\pi_L > \lambda_{HL}$, regime 1 cannot occur.

Figure 7.2 provides a graphical representation of the problem with auditing. On this figure, we have three points in the $(y, c)$ space. The consumption bundle for individuals of type $H$ is represented by $h$, where the slope of the indifference curve is 1. The distance between $h$ and the (no-tax) budget line $c = wz$ is the transfer that individuals of type $H$ have to pay. Point $l$ is the solution for individuals of type $L$ with a slope different from 1. We have represented the case where the slope is higher than 1, but it could have been less. Here, individuals $L$ are subject to a marginal subsidy and receive a transfer. Note the binding incentive constraint from $H$ to $L$ and the relative slope at $l$ of these two types indifference curves. Finally, $d$ is the solution for individuals of type $D$. The slope is 1 (no distortion as for individuals $H$); they receive a larger transfer than individuals $L$, and they also work less ($d$ is to the left of $l$). Yet note that with a positive marginal tax on $L$ and a weak income effect, it is not impossible to have $z_D > z_L$ in the second-best situation, especially in regime 1, where it is always the case. Finally, note that the indifference curve going through $l$ is a linear combination of the one going through $d$ and the one yielding a level of utility $\underline{u}$.

Equation (7.26) determines the optimal value of $\sigma$, which depends on both $k$, the cost of auditing, and $\underline{u}$ the penalty. Not surprisingly, the optimal audit probability (for type $D$ reports) is determined by the tradeoff between its negative effect on public expenditures $(-\mu\pi_D k)$ and its positive effect via the welfare gain stemming from a less stringent incentive-compatibility (IC) constraint.

### 7.4.4 Illustration: Paternalistic Objective

We use the same utility function as in section 7.3.4 and continue to assume $\underline{u} = 0$. However, to illustrate the pooling and the separating optima, we consider the following two scenarios for the parameter values:

|         | Scenario 1 | | | Scenario 2 | | |
|---------|------|------|------|------|------|------|
|         | *H*  | *L*  | *D*  | *H*  | *L*  | *D*  |
| $\alpha_i$ | 1    | 4    | 4    | 1    | 4    | 4    |
| $\pi_i$    | 0.6  | 0.07 | 0.33 | 0.6  | 0.2  | 0.2  |
| $w_i$      | 100  | 100  | 100  | 100  | 100  | 100  |

These two scenarios differ in the proportion of type $L$ and type $D$ within the economy. In scenario 1, there is a small proportion of type $L$ individuals, while this proportion is larger in scenario 2. In addition, we consider two audit technologies in terms of their cost: audit 1 is relatively expensive $(k(\sigma) = 2000\sigma^2)$, while audit 2 is cheaper $(k(\sigma) = 1000\sigma^2)$. The results are given in table 7.2 (scenario 1) and table 7.3 (scenario 2).

Not surprisingly, audit 1 implies lower audit probabilities than audit 2. In scenario 1, $\pi_L$ is relatively low so that without an audit a pooling optimum will occur with a positive marginal on $z_L$ and $z_D$. As in the case of the Paretian objective, audits increase from regime 1 to regime 2. In regime 1, lazy individuals will work less than the disabled, while in regime 2 they work more.

In scenario 2, the optimum without audit involves separation between individuals $D$ and $L$. This is because $\pi_L$ is now relatively high so that paternalistic considerations dominate. In this case, the second-best solution with and without audit involves no distortion on $z_D$, while a marginal subsidy is called for on $z_L$.

**Table 7.2**
Numerical example: Paternalistic objective, scenario 1

| Types | First-Best | | | No Audit | | |
|---|---|---|---|---|---|---|
| | $D$ | $L$ | $H$ | $D$ | $L$ | $H$ |
| $c$ | 86.74 | 86.74 | 86.74 | 57.72 | 57.72 | 94.04 |
| $z$ | 0.28 | 1.15 | 1.15 | 0.39 | 0.39 | 1.06 |
| $u$ | 4.29 | 1.80 | 3.79 | 3.74 | 3.74 | 3.97 |
| $T'(z)$ | 0 | $-3$ | 0 | 0.09 | 0.09 | 0 |

| Types | Audit 1 ($\pi = 0.04$, Regime 1) | | | Audit 2 ($\pi = 0.08$, Regime 2) | | |
|---|---|---|---|---|---|---|
| | $D$ | $L$ | $H$ | $D$ | $L$ | $H$ |
| $c$ | 65.35 | 54.05 | 91.55 | 68.06 | 53.70 | 90.59 |
| $z$ | 0.38 | 0.37 | 1.09 | 0.36 | 0.41 | 1.10 |
| $u$ | 3.88 | 3.71 | 3.92 | 3.95 | 3.63 | 3.89 |
| $T'(z)$ | 0.003 | 0.19 | 0 | 0 | 0.11 | 0 |

**Table 7.3**
Numerical example: Paternalistic objective, scenario 2

| Types | First-Best | | | No Audit | | |
|---|---|---|---|---|---|---|
| | $D$ | $L$ | $H$ | $D$ | $L$ | $H$ |
| $c$ | 92.19 | 92.19 | 92.19 | 52.20 | 70.07 | 97.8 |
| $z$ | 0.27 | 1.08 | 1.08 | 0.47 | 0.61 | 1.02 |
| $u$ | 4.37 | 2.17 | 3.93 | 3.49 | 3.49 | 4.06 |
| $T'(z)$ | 0 | $-3$ | 0 | 0 | $-0.71$ | 0 |

| Types | Audit 1 ($\pi = 0.12$, Regime 2) | | | Audit 2 ($\pi = 0.20$, Regime 2) | | |
|---|---|---|---|---|---|---|
| | $D$ | $L$ | $H$ | $D$ | $L$ | $H$ |
| $c$ | 60.54 | 70 | 95.67 | 67.20 | 71.50 | 94.42 |
| $z$ | 0.41 | 0.68 | 1.04 | 0.37 | 0.75 | 1.05 |
| $u$ | 3.76 | 3.31 | 4.01 | 3.93 | 3.13 | 3.98 |
| $T'(z)$ | 0 | $-0.91$ | 0 | 0 | $-1.15$ | 0 |

## 7.5   Interpretation

We have studied the design of retirement and disability benefits in a three-type setting. Healthy individuals have a low disutility of labor (continued activity). The two other types have identical preferences with a high disutility of labor. However, they differ in their (unobservable) health status. Type $L$ individuals have a high disutility for labor because they are leisure prone (or lazy). Type $D$ individuals, on the other hand, have a high disutility because they are disabled. We start from the premise that policymakers are not prepared to treat types $D$ and $L$ alike. Helping type $D$ individuals and allowing them to retire early with "generous" benefits is considered legitimate. However, society does not want to extend such a generous treatment to type $L$ individuals. Formally, this is introduced by considering either a (Paretian) social-welfare function (which puts relatively less weight on type $L$ individuals than on the others) or by using a paternalistic social-welfare function (which does not fully account for the type $L$ individual's disutility of labor).

In either setting, a first-best solution would imply earlier retirement for $D$ than for $L$ ($z_D < z_L$). However, when health status is not observable, it may or may not be possible to distinguish between the two types, so that the second-best solution may imply $z_D = z_L$. In that case, the effectiveness of disability benefits is severely undermined by the presence of the $L$ type, and the possibilities to help the disabled are limited. The situation can be improved if costly audits (tests for disabilities) become available. However, the second-best solution with an audit does not necessarily imply $z_D < z_L$. Surprisingly, we may even end up with a situation where the disabled retire later than the lazy ($z_D > z_L$).

Another interesting finding of our analysis is that the optimum often implies distorted retirement decisions, at least for types $L$ and $D$. However, in some situations there are no distortions, even in the second-best solution or where distortions affect only one of the types. We show that this depends on the pattern of binding incentive constraints, which in turn depends on how costly audits are.

To put these results in perspective, consider the policy implications of the NBER and OECD studies, which explain early retirement by a too extensive use of social insurance programs. They amount to making the overall system more neutral toward retirement decisions.[13]

Demographic aging makes such a reform extremely pressing. The problem with such a linear reform is that it is clearly legitimate because it regards workers who are not disabled or are not involuntarily unemployed. It makes economic sense to decrease the generosity of social insurance programs for those who abuse the system. However, for those who are truly disabled or unemployed, such a reform necessarily implies lower benefits, and this is questionable. From a public-finance viewpoint, the reform works. But from a social-welfare viewpoint, it is likely to be catastrophic.

What we show is that to avoid such an outcome, one should introduce or strengthen the audit and control techniques that allow the sorting out of leisure-prone workers and truly disabled individuals. In so doing, one can at the same time keep the disability benefits at a sufficient high level, while inducing the nondisabled to work a longer period of time. The same approach that is use with disability insurance can be used to deal with unemployment insurance.

### 7.6  Unemployment and Retirement

In this chapter, we thus far have been concerned with the welfare costs that nondisabled workers who pass for disabled impose on the whole of society and, in particular, on truly disabled workers. As has been shown in previous chapters, disability is not the only exit route to early retirement. Unemployment insurance is even more popular.[14] In this case, the issue is to sort out the truly unemployed workers from those who decide either on their own or by being pushed by their employers to quit the labor force and to benefit from unemployment compensation before reaching the age of retirement, when they are entitled to old-age pension benefits.

What we call *leisure-prone workers* can thus choose to become unemployed (even though unemployment compensation is not high) because employers give them a severance pay that makes up for the difference. In Belgium, this scheme is called "Canada Dry,"[15] since this way of pensioning people looks like an early retirement scheme but is not.

Using the same methodology as above, we could show that here again audits and controls can be socially desirable. Naturally, audits would address the "voluntary" character of unemployment.

Without going into the details, we now sketch the model we have in mind. Assume that there are two types of people, both with the same productivity $w$. The first type faces a probability $\pi$ of becoming unemployed after $z_0$ years. We label these individuals $U$ and those who keep their job $E$. These individuals know by age 0 and not $z_0$ whether they will be unemployed. The second type, denoted $L$, is made up of leisure-prone workers with a high disutility for work but with job security. For the sake of simplicity, we make two assumptions—no unemployment for the leisure-prone individuals and unemployment for the others known at the start.

We keep the same utility as above:

$$U_i = u(c_i) - \gamma_i \varphi(z_i),$$

with $\gamma_E = \gamma_U < \gamma_L$ and $z_U = z_0$. In the laissez-faire approach, $z_E > z_L > z_0$, $c_E = wz_E$, $c_L = wz_L$, and $c_U = wz_0$.

Introducing social weights $\psi_E = \psi_U > \psi_L$, first-best optimality implies $c_U = c_E > c_L$, $z_U > z_L > z_0$. If both $L$ and $E$ can mimic $U$, such an allocation is not sustainable. Following the same line of thinking as above, consider a scheme wherein individuals $E$ are prevented from mimicking both $L$ and $U$, who cannot be distinguished from each other. The next step is to allow for audits that make it possible to distinguish between $L$ and $U$. Not surprisingly, we can show that with not too costly audits, social welfare is increased, and in particular unemployment compensations can be raised.

## 7.7   Conclusion

In this chapter, we have presented an optimal scheme of social security that takes into account two important real-life dimensions. The first is that some workers cannot continue to work because of poor health; hence the need for disability insurance. The second is that for a number of cases of disability, it is costly to sort out those individuals who are truly disabled from those who are simply leisure prone. The conclusion is that the only way to avoid penalizing the truly disabled is either to introduce or strengthen audits and controls.

We have not presented a survey of the literature on disability insurance. In our setting, there is just one period of uncertainty, unlike Diamond and Mirrlees (1978, 1986, 2004), who consider a continuous-time model where representative individuals face a given probability of becoming disabled at any time. Here, the government does not observe disability, which makes mimicking possible. It designs a disability insurance scheme that induces healthy workers to stop working and that is such that the payroll tax decreases with age while disability benefits increase with age.

There is another difference: in our setting, audits are perfect. Diamond and Sheshinski (1995) study disability insurance with costly and imperfect audits. Their optimal scheme includes three types of bundles (benefits + contributions): one for able agents who continue working, one for the truly disabled, and one for the disabled who have not been tagged as such (with lower benefits than the disability benefits).

It is clear that these two features—imperfect audits and evolving information as to disability—are important features of a complete disability insurance scheme. However, these features bring analytical difficulties that are outside the scope of this book. In spite of these differences, we end up with the same conclusion as these authors. In other words, disability insurance—particularly when auditing is loose, for whatever reasons—may explain part of the decline in the activity rate of elderly workers, as studied by Parsons (1980, 1991, 1996) and Bound (1989, 1991).

# 8        The Demand Side

This book's explanation of early retirement thus far has rested on the supply side of the labor market. Elderly workers decide to exit from work because they find it financially attractive. But factors on the demand side for labor also may contribute to the decline of labor-force participation of older workers. First, low-skilled older workers may exhibit a declining relative productivity in times of rapid technological change and become unalluring to employers. Second, insufficient training may contribute to declining productivity. Third, rigid age-earnings profiles that are caused by specific institutional arrangements (like high minimum wages or stringent employment-protection legislation) reduce the employment opportunities of the older unemployed. Fourth, temporary negative demand shocks may lead to irreversible labor-force withdrawal. As indicated, some of the demand-side influences tend to reinforce each other. For instance, if wages do not sufficiently respond to lower productivity, demand for older workers declines, and unemployment increases.

So far, the roles of employers and of public authorities have not been taken into account in our analysis. Yet it is known that employers have been very active in retiring their labor force early, particularly when earnings increase with seniority or, more precisely, when the gap between earnings and productivity increases with age. At the same time, public authorities have been induced to push old workers out of the labor force with the hope of freeing jobs for unemployed youth. Thus, costly seniority rules and youth unemployment are generally invoked to explain early retirement. Note that these explanations do not contradict the above approach. High implicit taxes on postponed activity can be found in countries with youth unemployment and with seniority-based pay.

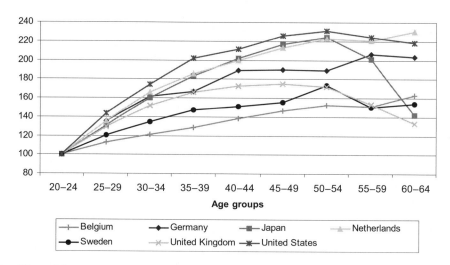

**Figure 8.1**
Earnings profiles in some OECD countries
*Source: OECD Labour Market Statistics* (2002).
*Note:* Average gross earnings of full-time workers in various age groups. Earnings of workers age 20 to 24 are normalized to 100. Data for Belgium and Sweden were collected in 1994 and for all other countries 1996.

In this chapter, we deal with these two questions in turn. We first present Lazear's (1979, 1981) argument that for incentive reasons firms pay workers first below their productivity and then above. We look at some empirical evidence of such a divergence between wage and productivity profiles. We then look at why governments would choose to push elderly workers out of the labor force to free jobs for unemployed youth.

Before proceeding, let us look at figure 8.1, which provides wage profiles for a number of European countries.[1] A greater use of seniority-based pay can be observed in, for example, the United States and the Netherlands than in Belgium and Sweden. But in the United States and Sweden, the average retirement age is relatively high, while it is low in Belgium and the Netherlands. Furthermore, although the incentive for workers to stay in the labor market should be stronger in the United States and the Netherlands due to significantly increasing earnings at higher ages, only in the Netherlands does the low effective retirement age confirm this suspicion. The opposite is true for Belgium and Sweden. This demonstrates that considerations of only the supply side do not reveal all determinants of the retirement process.[2] For the whole story, we have to look at the demand side and determine whether productivity follows through. Moreover, it is not clear whether seniority-based pay induces early retirement or vice versa. One could argue either that firms with seniority-based pay will push their governments to adopt generous exit routes or that countries with early retirement incentives generate steep age-wage profiles.

## 8.1  The Lazear Model

Lazear (1979, 1981) provides a theory of deferred compensation as a motivator for workers to stay with a firm as they grow old. He argues that senior workers receive high wages less because they are worth what they are paid during their senior years and more because high wages motivate them during the early years of their careers. Since the young want to grow old in the firm and to reap the benefits of high-wage jobs, they put forth higher levels of effort than they would for flat wages. The theory is illustrated in figure 8.2.

Let us denote $w(t)$ as the worker's wage at time $t$ and $v(t)$ as his marginal value product. Let $w_R$ be the minimum wage that would induce the worker to keep being employed. The reservation wage reflects the opportunity cost of working and includes elements such as preference for leisure, health, informal work, and so on. The reservation wage would be expected to rise with age. Time $z$ is the date of voluntary and efficient retirement. If the worker received a compensation according to his productivity profile $v(t)$, he would choose to retire voluntarily at time $z$ because at that point the alternative use of time equals the worker's marginal product or payment.

In a competitive setting with perfect capital markets and full information, the worker would be indifferent between any wage profiles whose present value is equal to the present value of the marginal-value product. Thus, he would agree to any employment contract where

$$\int_0^z [w(t) - v(t)]e^{-rt}\, dt = 0, \tag{8.1}$$

where $r$ is the constant discount rate and $z$ the age of retirement. In a competitive market, a spot-market equilibrium would also be expected:

$w(t) = v(t).$

Yet this equality is rarely observed. Instead, a scissors effect can be seen: the productivity curve begins above the wage curve, intersects

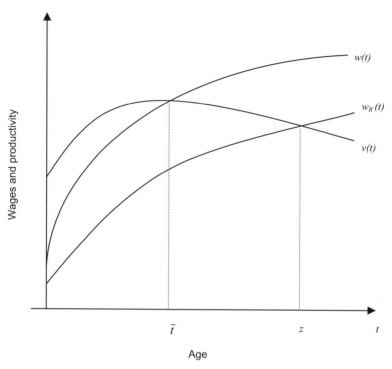

**Figure 8.2**
The Lazear theory of defined compensation

with the wage curve, and finally moves below the wage curve. Lazear explains this scissors effect as resulting from agency considerations.[3] The worker's effort is not observable and can be monitored only at some cost. The most effective weapon at the employer's disposal is the threat of dismissal, which would not be effective with wages equal to marginal product. To make the dismissal threat credible, Lazear suggests deferring pay toward the end of the work career. Suppose that a worker would be paid according to his productivity profile $v(t)$ and is approaching his retirement date $z$. At that point, the incentives to shirk become overwhelming. If he shirks, the worst thing that can possibly happen is that he gets fired. If he gets fired, he does not receive wage $w(t) = v(t)$ during the next period, but he does get to enjoy the value of his leisure, which is equal to his wage at time $z$. Thus, nothing is lost by shirking. If, instead, the worker were paid a wage profile $w(t)$ as it is outlined in figure 8.1, then things would be different. Under such circumstances, shirking allows him to enjoy the value of his leisure $w_R(t)$ during the next period, but he risks forgoing wage $w(t)$. Since $w(t)$ is set such that it is well above $v(t)$ at time $z$, a worker would forfeit quasi rents by shirking. Thus, the sufficiently steep $w$-profile induces workers to perform at a higher level of effort than they would if they were paid their marginal product at each point in their careers.

Note that in figure 8.2 we have not introduced any social security programs or mandatory retirement age. Workers retire at age $z$ because at that age and from then on working one more year returns less than retiring does. It is clear that introducing social security and its underlying implicit taxation will make the $w_R(t)$ curve shift upward and thus allow earlier retirement.

Important in our context is that a wage profile that slopes upward more strongly than the productivity profile introduces a new source of inefficiency, since firms have an incentive to encourage workers to retire early. The firm would profit from terminating the worker's labor contract before time $z$. It would be optimal for the firm to terminate all workers at time $\bar{t}$ when the workers' marginal productivity begins to fall short of wages. Hence, firms may have a tendency to lay off older workers in mutual agreement by paying them a severance pay at the amount of the difference between their last salary and the unemployment benefit provided by the government. The combination of severance pay and unemployment compensation is negotiable between workers and employers. Hence, the firm profits from this arrangement if the severance pay is lower than what the firm saves by dismissing the older worker, which is the difference between wage and productivity. This condition is met if the unemployment compensation from the government is high enough. Thus, both firm and worker can share in the rent that early retirement programs offer to them.

The key prediction of this model is that wages rise more rapidly than marginal product. In the following, we review the empirical evidence for this constellation.

## 8.2   Empirical Evidence

Some empirical studies that were published after Lazear's (1979) work concluded that differences in wages were not due to differences in marginal productivity. Lazear and Moore (1984) and Oliviera, Cohn, and Kiker (1989) circumvent the difficulty of measuring directly productivity profiles of employees by assuming that the labor earnings of a self-employed worker can be attributed closely to his value of marginal productivity, since they have no incentive to shirk. Therefore, wages of the self-employed may be regarded as a good measure of the productivity on an otherwise comparable private employee. Using U.S. data from 1978, Lazear and Moore (1984) compare the observable productivity profile of self-employed persons (their actual earnings) with the observable wage profile of employees. They find that the slope of the wage profile of the employees is larger than the slope for the self-employed and argue that this is an incentive effect: employers raise the slopes of the age-earnings profile to induce their employees to work harder and to abstain from shirking near their retirement age. Oliviera, Cohn, and Kiker (1989) have drawn data from a household survey of income dynamics conducted by the University of Michigan. They show that at an early stage of tenure in a firm (approximately six years) workers tend to receive wages higher than their productivity. During a second stage of approximately 12 years, productivity exceeds earnings. And beyond that point, wages are again higher than productivity and remain fairly constant even as productivity declines. The authors claim that at this stage, employers may be reluctant to lower a worker's wage, or institutional arrangements (such as union contracts and job tenure agreements) mitigate against wage reduction. Furthermore, "this gap also explains, at least in part, why many employers are eager to offer attractive early retirement plans for their employees" (Oliviera, Cohn, and Kiker, 1989, p. 10). Kotlikoff and Gokhale (1992) confirm Lazear's theoretical conjectures by adopting another approach to measure productivity. They estimate the age-productivity relationship for a single firm using the first-order condition that the present expected value of total compensation equals the present expected value of productivity. Hence, the parameters of the age-productivity relationship can be identified from information on how total present expected compensation varies with age. The data in the study are earnings histories for over 300,000 employees of a Fortune 1,000 corporation covering the period 1969 through 1983. The results indicate that productivity declines with age and that workers are paid more than they produce when old to offset being paid less than they produce when young. For some occupation and sex groups, the difference between productivity and compensation at young and old ages is sizable. Lazear (1999) presents new evidence from data on a large autoglass-installing firm that is headquartered in Ohio (United States). The study examined detailed records of weekly output for each installer in the company from January 1994 through July 1995. The data on output per week and compensation per week were used to estimate the relation of both productivity and pay to tenure. The results show that irrespective of the specification, the tenure coefficient in the pay regression is higher than the tenure coefficient in the output regression.

A new and more satisfactory approach was undertaken by Hellerstein and Neumark (1995) using Israeli data and Hellerstein, Neumark, and Troska (1999) using U.S. data. The basic difficulty is in measuring productivity differences. Their approach consisted of using a dataset that matched firm-level data and employee characteristics. They estimated marginal productivity differentials between workers of different ages by applying a production-function approach to firms' technologies. Then they modeled the wage structure of the same firms to estimate earnings differentials between workers of different ages. The results show that both earnings and productivity profiles are upward sloping. Most important, the estimated age-earnings and age-productivity profiles mirror each other closely and are statistically indistinguishable. But because the estimated productivity profiles are relatively imprecise, the authors concede that they do not have strong evidence against the configuration of the Lazear argument.

Whereas most recent studies in the United States show that seniority in wage equations reflects human-capital accumulation, a number of European studies show that wages rise more quickly than productivity. Hoegeland and Klette (1999) for Norway as well as Crepon, Deniau, and Perez-Duarte (2002, 2003) for France show that the age profile of wages exhibits an increasingly concave pattern while the age profile of productivity stops rising and even decreases after some experience level. Crepon, Deniau, and Perez-Duarte (2002a, 2002b) have adopted the new approach provided by Hellerstein, Neumark, and Troska (1999), based on the joint estimation of a wage equation and a production function that leads to direct comparisons of wage and productivity differentials. They use a dataset that matches firm-level data with employee characteristics in France. It covers the period 1994 through 1997 and consists of 77,868 firms. Figure 8.3 displays their result that the wage-productivity gap increases with age. For workers age 35 and over, the increase in wages cannot be interpreted as reflecting human-capital accumulation. The result that wage profiles rise more quickly than productivity profiles can be shown to persist by robustness checks across time periods, industries, and identifying

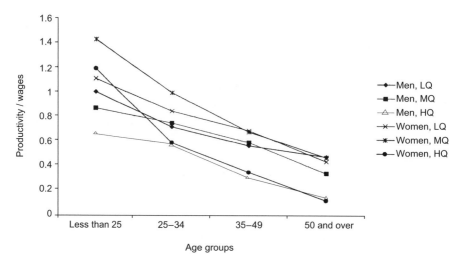

**Figure 8.3**
Wage-productivity gap in French services according to age, gender, and skill
*Source:* Crepon, Deniau, and Perez-Duarte (2002a, 2002b).

assumptions. The authors conclude that this finding is consistent with the implementation of an early retirement policy in France that helped to remove older workers from the labor market.

Using personnel data from a large Italian firm, Flabbi and Ichino (2001) test whether a upward-sloping wage profile reflects the higher productivity of senior workers. If this were true, the observation of an effect of seniority on wages would depend on the presence of controls for individual productivity. As productivity indicators, they take job-performance ratings made by immediate supervisors. Because this indicator has been determined to be a good measure of individual productivity, they add two further indicators in their estimation—absenteeism and reported misconduct episodes. Their results are unambiguous: performance indicators have no effect on the seniority-wage profile. Although tenure increases the worker's ranking in the distribution of wages, it reduces his or her ranking in the distribution of these performance indicators. Only at the lowest levels of the firm's hierarchy is there evidence that productivity drives at least partially the relationship between wages and seniority. At all other levels, the authors conclude that their results provide evidence against explanations that claim that greater productivity is a driving force for the wage-seniority profile. Instead, alternative explanations like Lazear's deferred-compensation theory are more likely to explain the observed evidence.

Taking a similar approach, Dohmen (2003) uses personnel data from the Dutch national aircraft manufacturer Fokker. He also comes to the conclusion that seniority-wage profiles are largely independent of controls for reported performance in cross-sectional wage regressions. The author explains this result by the rigidity of nominal wages: whereas performance improvements may trigger wage raises, deteriorated performance ratings do not cause wages to fall. Because of this asymmetry, two identical workers with the same job assignment, performance rating, and earnings history may receive identical wages even though one worker's last evaluation score has fallen. So differences in wage and productivity profiles can be explained by institutional rigidities in the pay policies of firms.

Summarizing the empirical studies, there seems to be some evidence (at least in European countries) that the wage profile rises above the productivity profile at the end of a working life. Older workers tend to receive wages that are higher than the value of their marginal product. This evidence provides the background for an explanation of why firms may have an incentive to induce older workers to retire early. In most cases, such arrangements between employers and employees require the support of explicit or implicit public early retirement programs, such as unemployment benefits for older workers. Employers and older workers benefit from such arrangements, but they are doing so at the expense of taxpayers who have to finance the public early retirement programs. In the following section, we investigate the motives of governments for engaging in such early retirement bargaining at the burden of taxpayers.

## 8.3   Early Retirement and Macroeconomic Performance

Early retirement policies also have been motivated by employment considerations. Facing unemployment problems in declining sectors, governments have long implemented soft landing programs to reduce labor supply. Their programs are restricted to a number of industries or even firms. Workers have a strong incentive to accept a deal, the generosity of which has varied over time. Another motivation for a more general early retirement policy is to free jobs for younger unemployed workers. Such a policy suits firms as well but is implemented at the expenses of taxpayers.

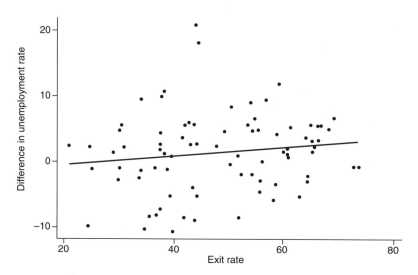

**Figure 8.4**
Exit rates of men born 1931 through 1940 and changes in unemployment rates of men
age 21 through 30, 1991 through 1996
*Source:* Boldrin, Dolado, Jimeno, and Perrachi (1999).

Theoretically, an extremely naive model of unemployment is needed
to generate such an outcome—namely, one early retiree implies one
job for the young unemployed. Boldrin, Dolado, Jimeno, and Perrachi
(1999) have tested this policy on labor-market data for European countries over the period 1986 through 1996. They look for empirical support of the thesis that a decrease in the rate of participation of aged
workers generates reduced unemployment among younger cohorts.
Figure 8.4 plots the relationship between the exit rates from the labor
force of older workers (age 50 and over) and the variation in the unemployment rates among young workers (age 21 through 30). If the
policy were successful, we would have to expect a negative relationship. The estimates of Boldrin, Dolado, Jimeno, and Perrachi (1999) do
not show evidence of a negative correlation for men or for women (not
shown here). Controlling for cohort effects or using different lags did
not change these results. Hence, the early retirement of older workers
does not induce lower youth unemployment.

One simple reason for the failure of policies that induce earlier retirement to reduce youth unemployment may be that the central assumption underlying such a policy is wrong—that if firms lay off an old

worker, they will hire instead a young worker. This conjecture finds no corroboration in the empirical literature. The econometric evidence on substitution patterns for workers of different ages is not at all homogeneous enough to allow for such policy implications.

Mitchell and Levine (1988) estimate a demand system for heterogeneous labor to evaluate the impact of the aging of the baby-boom generation on the relative wages of older versus younger men and women. The estimates show substantial substitution as well as complementarity across workers of different age. One result reveals that older female employees (age 55 and over) were substitutes for mature men (age 35 through 54). At the same time, older male employees were estimated to be complementary workers with young men (age 20 through 34). Surveys of further empirical literature have been provided by Hamermesh (1986, 1993). The results are quite heterogeneous, although some evidence can be found suggesting that workers of different ages are substitutes. In three studies, adult women are found to be substitutes for young workers. But these results have to be taken with great caution and are not at all conventional wisdom. Most studies estimate whether workers at different ages are substitutes in production. This substitution effect means that for a given level of output an increase in the cost of employment of older workers induces employers to increase their demand for young workers and to substitute them for older workers. But there is also a scale effect. The higher cost of employment of older workers provides employers with an incentive to decrease employment of all inputs, including younger workers. The magnitude of the scale effect depends on the elasticity of product demand with respect to price; the larger this elasticity is, the larger the scale effect will be. If the scale effect is larger than the substitution effect, then workers at different ages may turn out to be gross complements, even though the production elasticity estimated them to be substitutes. Finally, Hebbink (1993) finds that the demand for young and old workers changes in the same direction if one of their wages changes. In other words, old and young labor are complementary factors of production.

All in all, there is no need to assume that old and young workers are gross substitutes. Instead, there are good reasons to assume that firms will substitute old workers against capital or rationalize production. Labor is, in general, a substitute for each other large aggregate input that has been defined in studies of production (Hamermesh, 1993,

p. 105). This conclusion holds especially for production workers. If this is true, any policy that provides public early retirement programs to alleviate the dismissal of old workers is counterproductive if it relies on a behavior of firms that is supposed to substitute young for old workers. The undesirable consequence will be that total unemployment increases along with the taxes that finance unemployment benefits.

# 9    Conclusion

This chapter presents several policy recommendations and salient issues that will surely be explored in the near future.

## 9.1   Policy Recommendations

Our societies are aging. This has an unavoidable effect on the financial viability of social security programs that are aimed at providing support for the elderly. Aging is a demographic phenomenon when it pertains to the decline in fertility (particularly when this decline follows a temporary uprise, as in the sequence of baby boom and baby bust) and to the increase in life expectancy. Aging is an economic phenomenon when it concerns the rapid withdrawal from the labor force of legions of older workers and an ever-decreasing effective age of retirement.

In this book, we are concerned with the issue of early retirement because it is an economic issue and a trend that might be able to be reversed. Increased longevity is a desirable trend that escapes economic explanation.

In the early 1960s, the work-force participation rate for people age 60 and over was above 70 percent everywhere and approached 80 percent in several countries. By the end of the 1990s, this rate had fallen to below 20 percent in countries such as Belgium, Italy, France, and the Netherlands. If this downward labor-force trend and the expected upward longevity trend were to continue, there would be no way that our pension and health systems could survive.

To reverse the trend toward early retirement, it is important to understand its determinants. The reasons generally invoked include economic growth, increased preference for leisure, employers' choice, social security provisions, labor legislation, and difficult working conditions. The view adopted in this book is that a large proportion of early retirement decisions can be explained by social security and legislation. The demand-side factors—such as the desire of unions to free jobs for young unemployed workers and employers' objective to get rid of older workers considered too expensive for what they produce— are also important. But these factors simply explain why social security and labor legislation penalize a postponement of retirement.

For us, the conclusion seems obvious. Let us reform social security programs—including old-age pensions, disability insurance, and unemployment insurance—so that older workers who are able to continue working are induced to do so. As we have seen in many countries (notably in France and Germany) where people retire very early, people like the system as it is, and there is a lot of resistance to reforms that are aimed at raising the age of retirement. This means that reforms have to be carefully prepared and explained to the public. People have to be reassured that these reforms are aimed at making the pension system sustainable and therefore that they and their children will benefit from them.

On the priority list of reforms, the idea is to make the pension system actuarially as neutral as possible—not in the aggregate but at the margin. Total neutrality is not possible in a setting where the government wants to do some redistribution when there is asymmetric information. Even though unemployment insurance and disability insurance have often been used as pathways to retirement by workers who were neither truly unemployed nor disabled, these two types of social insurance need to be kept at the same level of generosity as they are now. Cutting their replacement rates at earlier ages to make them less attractive would be a mistake. The right course of action is to increase and improve the monitoring devices to sort out the truly disabled and unemployed from the other elderly workers who merely want to enjoy retiring early at little cost to themselves.

Finally, there is much to do on the demand side of the labor market. First of all, it would be useful to reduce the gap between wages and productivity in old age. This would curtail the current incentive to lay off older workers. Second, government and unions ought to admit that forced early retirement does not contribute to the employment of the young unemployed. Third, countries such as Germany and France should adopt a more flexible view of the job market and accept the idea that there can be more than one career in a lifetime. Fourth, a training structure needs to help all workers, including the aged ones, to update their knowledge and to change jobs. Finally, the current sharp divide that now exists between work and retirement could be replaced by partial and progressive retirement or even by work after retirement. In that respect, a current-earnings test[1] should be reformed to create a balance between the freedom to work after retirement and the withholding of noncontributory pensions from individuals who are still earning a living.

The objection could be made that things are changing and that our concerns are less relevant today than they were a decade ago. Indeed, the most recent data suggest that the rate of labor-force activity of older workers has stopped declining and is even increasing in a number of countries. Some programs, particularly sectorial early retirement ones, have been abandoned, and the old-age-pension retirement age has been raised. Although these trends show that at last things seem to be moving in the right direction, they should not hide the fact that we are still a long way from reaching a solution. With life expectancy increasing by one year every five years, much higher increases in the effective age of retirement are needed than those we observe in countries such as Germany and France. Also, for reforms to be effective, they must be comprehensive. Merely closing one door to early exit from the job market is not enough. All doors need to be closed, and for this kind of legislation political courage is needed.

## 9.2   Salient Issues for Future Research

This book presents a number of theoretical and policy issues that pertain to the relationship between social security and retirement decisions. The issues selected are not comprehensive but correspond to the interests of the authors. Some of the issues not presented have been treated elsewhere, and other issues have not yet been fully thought through. We can trust that they are on the agenda of a number of researchers.

### 9.2.1   Retirement and Portability

Labor mobility in the European Union is still very low in absolute terms but also relative to interstate mobility in the United States. One reason for this lack of mobility is the lack of portability of pensions, both public and private. Yet an increase in mobility can be expected as the current shift from defined-benefit plans to defined-contribution schemes continues. The question to raise at this point concerns the implications of this trend on retirement patterns. At first sight, defined-benefit schemes seem to induce some workers to retire early,

even though they would be ready to move to another country and enjoy additional years of activity.

### 9.2.2   Flexible Retirement and Second Careers

In countries with early retirement practices, there is little upward flexibility. In other words, workers can retire well before the normal age of
retirement but not after. Furthermore, the choices that do exist are of
the all-or-nothing type. It would be interesting to foster reforms that
lead to more flexibility and study their expected incidence. One that
has been discussed here consists of making social security actuarially
neutral: anyone who retires before the normal age of retirement may
do so, but he or she receives a lower annual benefit; anyone who
works beyond the age of retirement is allowed to do so with pension
benefits that are increased accordingly. Second, it should be possible
to opt for work weeks that decline in hours over time to avoid an
all too often painful crash landing from activity to retirement. Third,
many firms will still insist on getting rid of their employers after a certain age. The possibility of a second career (which exists in Japan and
in Finland) should then be considered. These are policy recommendations that should be supported by further research on the issue of flexible retirement.[2]

### 9.2.3   Heterogeneity in Life Expectancy

Most social security models assume identical longevity, except for
the differences between men and women. But many other differences
develop—some at birth and others as life goes on. These differences
affect labor-market incentives and retirement choices. A social security
system that is too rigid, with mandatory annuitization at a given age,
entails all sorts of redistribution that are not all desirable. Thus, there
can be a good case made for flexibility and for not having earnings
tests.[3]

### 9.2.4   Nonstandard Models

Economists are increasingly open to models of savings and retirement
behavior that involve time inconsistency. After all, myopia was one of
the first reasons invoked to explain mandatory pension systems. As the
seminal paper of Diamond and Köszegi (2003) shows, this is a fertile
area for research.

# Notes

## Chapter 1

1. Herbertsson and Orszag (2003).

## Chapter 2

1. Disability pensions that are outside the old-age pension scheme can be received at ages earlier than 60. But the number of people who receive this type of pension is negligible compared to the number of old-age pensioners.

## Chapter 3

1. See Gruber and Wise (1999a, pp. 385, 422).

2. See Gruber and Wise (1999a, pp. 54, 259).

3. See Gruber and Wise (1999a, p. 456).

4. For a survey of literature before 1999, see Lumsdaine and Mitchell (1999).

## Chapter 4

1. See also Hu (1979), Fields and Mitchell (1984), Breyer and Straub (1993), and Diamond (2003).

2. In chapter 6, this assumption is dropped.

3. $P_t^i$ is the overall (gross) pension wealth. The flow of pension is obtained by dividing it by the number of years in retirement: $1 - z_t^i$.

4. This is an important point: a mandatory, contributive, fully funded pension system can entail big distortions that can be justified in the name of paternalism. Accordingly, government can force myopic individuals to save by convincing them that this is what their true selves really want. For more on this, see O'Donoghue and Rabin (1999).

5. If yearly pensions $\bar{p}$ increase with the age of retirement $z$, a third effect counteracting these two burdens enters the implicit tax formula.

6. Notional accounts are a scheme of individual retirement accounts. They are not funded per se but nevertheless represent individualized claims on future public resources. The idea is that these notional accounts mimic a private defined contribution system of individualized accounts, with the "return" on such accounts explicitly linked by law to a formula that takes account of current and prospective demographic and productivity change.

7. Both marginal utilities $u_c$ and $u_d$ are decreasing with earnings.

8. Here total and substitution effects are the same (zero income effect).

9. We come back to this point in chapter 5, section 5.5.

10. An important literature deals with these two points—(1) the impossibility of a Pareto-improving shift from a pay-as-you-go plan to a fully fund plan in a distortionless world and (2) the possibility of Pareto-improving reform when distortions are not justified by, for example, distributive objectives. See Breyer (1989), Brunner (1996), Fenge (1995), and Belan and Pestieau (1999).

11. Some long-term-care programs are subject to tests of the insuree's means and also of his children's.

12. On this, see Cremer, Lozachmeur, and Pestieau (2003, 2004a, 2004b, 2004c).

13. See chapter 8.

## Chapter 5

1. This chapter is heavily based on joint research that was conducted with Georges Casamatta and Helmuth Cremer. See Casamatta, Cremer, and Pestieau (2004, 2005).

2. More recent Eurobarometers show the same pattern of answers.

3. European Commission (2003).

4. See European Commission (2003) and Boeri (2004).

5. For more on this, see Cremer and Pestieau (2003).

6. Dellis, Desmet, Jousten, and Perelman (2004) and Desmet, Jousten, Perelman, and Pestieau (2003).

7. We follow Fernandez and Rodrik (1991).

8. In this subsection, for clarity reasons, we use subscripts for denoting individuals.

## Chapter 6

1. See, e.g., Burbidge (1983).

2. This chapter is in large part based on Michel and Pestieau (2000, 2003).

3. Unlike Hu, we do not introduce a bequest motive in our modeling because it does not seem relevant to the problem considered. See also Kotlikoff and Summers (1979).

4. A number of authors have argued that the observed decline in the effective age of retirement is due mainly to the tax on prolonged activity, which varies a lot across countries. See chapter 3, the earlier work of Feldstein (1974) and Boskin (1977), and very recently the international comparisons of Gruber and Wise (1999a) and Blöndal and Scarpetta (1998a, 1998b).

5. Separability is not needed here.

6. We assume here that the pension level is independent of the age of retirement. A more general approach would be to define the overall pension benefits by $(1 - \alpha z)p$. Then an increase of z implies a tax equal to $\tau_w + \alpha p / w$, which is labeled in the literature (e.g., Gruber and Wise, 1999a) as the implicit tax on postponed activity. This approach would make the analytics more difficult without bringing more insights. See also chapter 4.

7. Actually, $\tau_{r0}$ acts as a lump-sum tax.

8. $\dfrac{\partial \tilde{d}}{\partial \omega} = \dfrac{\partial d}{\partial \omega} - qz \dfrac{\partial d}{\partial \omega_0}$;   $\dfrac{\partial \tilde{d}}{\partial q} = \dfrac{\partial d}{\partial q} + \dfrac{s}{q} \dfrac{\partial d}{\partial \omega_0}$;

$\dfrac{\partial \tilde{z}}{\partial \omega} = \dfrac{\partial z}{\partial \omega} - qz \dfrac{\partial z}{\partial \omega_0}$;   $\dfrac{\partial \tilde{z}}{\partial q} = \dfrac{\partial z}{\partial q} + \dfrac{s}{q} \dfrac{\partial z}{\partial \omega_0}$.

## Chapter 7

1. This chapter is based on joint research that was conducted with Helmuth Cremer and Jean-Marie Lozachmeur. See Cremer, Lozachmeur, and Pestieau (2003, 2004a, 2004c).

2. Again, we use the subscripts to denote individual types.

3. We use the term *actuarial neutrality* (or fairness) regarding retirement. This has to be distinguished from *fairness* (marginal or average) regarding the return from saving—namely, the relation between contribution and benefit. For more on this, see Crawford and Lilien (1981) and Desmet and Jousten (2004). See also chapter 4.

4. Each type can potentially mimic either of the two other types.

5. That is, when any bundles $(c_L, z_L)$ and $(c_D, z_D)$ satisfying (7.11) are permitted. We do not prove this property here since it can be most easily obtained from the results in the next section.

6. An alternative method, considered by Marchand, Pestieau, and Racionero (2003), is to observe the consumption vectors of both types, which surely will reveal their differences. On that basis, one can self-select the two types with a solution that can be implemented with nonlinear taxes on consumption and income.

7. There is some literature on this. In general, the tests are imperfect, generating errors of types 1 and 2. See Diamond and Sheshinski (1995) and Parsons (1996).

8. These first-order conditions also apply to the case where $\sigma = 0$—that is, there is no audit but we do not *a priori* impose pooling between L and D. They can be used to show that with $\pi = 0$, pooling is unavoidable. To see this, recall that without an audit, L and D are on the same indifference curve. A simple graphical argument shows that we have $\lambda_{HL} > 0$ and $\lambda_{HD} = 0$ when $z_L > z_D$, while we have $\lambda_{HD} > 0$ and $\lambda_{HL} = 0$ when $z_D > z_L$. However, when $\lambda_{HL} > 0$ and $\lambda_{HD} = 0$, we have from (7.14) and (7.15) that $z_L$ is distorted downward while $z_D$ is not distorted. But with both types on the same indifference curve,

this implies $z_D > z_L$, and we have a contradiction. The case where $\lambda_{HD} > 0$ and $\lambda_{HL} = 0$ can be dealt with along the same lines.

9. To be more precise, the mimicked individual would be hurt as much as the mimicker. Consequently, a distortion cannot be welfare-improving.

10. For the sake of illustration, we assume that the individuals $H$ remain on the same indifference curve without and with an audit. In general, this will not be true.

11. Regime 1 yields a similar representation, except that $D$ now faces a distortion.

12. If the first-best allocation described in section 7.3.1 respects $(HL)$, then the first-best allocation is implementable with audits. If it is not (which is the case if $\psi_L$ is high enough), then $(HL)$ would bind with free audit.

13. See Desmet, Jousten, Perelman, and Pestieau (2003) and Desmet and Jousten (2004).

14. The Dutch would be more concerned by abuses of disability insurance, and the Belgian by abuses of unemployment compensations.

15. It refers to an old commercial for Canada Dry ginger ale, which claimed that the soft drink "has the color of beer, looks like beer, but is not beer."

## Chapter 8

1. Further evidence for increasing and concave wage profiles over the life cycle—differentiated by gender and education—can be found in Blöndal, Field, and Girouard (2002).

2. In fact, a study by Duval (2003) shows that factors on the supply side like the implicit tax rate and standard retirement ages are found to explain only a third of the trend decline in the labor-force participation of older males in OECD countries over the last three decades. This suggests that greater attention should be paid to factors on the demand side of the labor market.

3. Another reason that wage profiles would be steeper than productivity profiles can be found in Carmichael (1983). His argument uses a human-capital model and is based on specific training within a firm.

## Chapter 9

1. See Cremer, Lozachmeur, and Pestieau (2004a).

2. See Simonovits (2004).

3. Diamond (2002).

# References

Anderson, K. H., and R. V. Burkhauser. (1985). The retirement-health nexus: A new measure of an old puzzle. *Journal of Human Ressources*, 20(3): 315–330.

Assous, L. (2001). Les opinions des Français au début 2000 en matière d'âge de départ à la retraite. *Etudes et Résultats*, 150. Paris: Ministère de l'Emploi.

Atkinson, A. B., and A. Sandmo. (1980). Welfare implications of the taxation of savings. *Economic Journal*, 90: 529–549.

Bazzoli, G. J. (1985). The early retirement decision: New empirical evidence on the influence of health. *Journal of Human Resources*, 20(2): 214–234.

Belan, P., and P. Pestieau. (1999). Privatizing social security: A critical assessment. *Geneva Papers on Risk and Insurance: Issues and Practice*, 24: 114–130.

Blöndal, S., S. Field, and N. Girouard. (2002). Investment in human capital through upper-secondary and tertiary education. *OECD Economic Studies*, 34: 41–89.

Blöndal, S., and S. Scarpetta. (1998a). *Falling Participation Rates among Older Workers in the OECD Countries*. Paris: OECD.

Blöndal, S., and S. Scarpetta. (1998b). *The Retirement Decision in OECD Countries*. Working Paper 202, OECD, Paris.

Blundell, R., C. Meghir, and S. Smith. (2002). Pension incentives and the pattern of early retirement. *Economic Journal*, 112: 153–170.

Boeri, T. (2004). Pension reforms in Europe. Unpublished manuscript.

Boeri, T., A. Börsch-Supan, and G. Tabellini. (2000). Would you like to shrink the welfare state? *Economic Policy*, 32: 7–50.

Boeri, T., A. Börsch-Supan, and G. Tabellini. (2002). Pension reforms and the opinion of European citizens. *American Economic Review: Papers and Proceedings*, 92: 396–401.

Boldrin, M., J. J. Dolado, J. F. Jimeno, and F. Perrachi. (1999). The future of pensions in Europe. *Economic Policy*, 29: 289–320.

Boskin, M. J. (1977). Social security and retirement decisions. *Economic Enquiry*, 15: 1–25.

Boskin, M. J., and M. D. Hurd. (1978). The effect of social security on early retirement. *Journal of Public Economics*, 10: 361–377.

Bound, J. (1991). Self-reported versus objective measures of health in retirement models. *Journal of Human Ressources*, 26(1): 106–138.

Bound, J. (1989). The health and earnings of rejected disability insurance applicants. *American Economic Review*, 79: 482–503.

Bound, J. (1991). The health and earnings of a rejected disability insurance applicant: Reply. *American Economic Review*, 81: 1427–1434.

Bound, J., M. Schoenbaum, T. R. Stinebrickner, and T. Waidmann. (1999). The dynamic effects of health on the labor-force transitions of older workers. *Labour Economics*, 6: 179–202.

Breyer, F. (1989). On the intergenerational Pareto efficiency of pay-as-you-go financial pension systems. *Journal of Institutional and Theoretical Economics*, 145: 643–658.

Breyer, F., and M. Straub. (1993). Welfare effects of unfunded pension systems when labor supply is endogeneous. *Journal of Public Economics*, 50: 77–91.

Brunner, J. K. (1996). Transition from a pay-as-you-go to a fully funded pension systems: The case of differing individuals and intragenerational fairness. *Journal of Public Economics*, 60: 131–146.

Burbidge, J. B. (1983). Social security and savings plans in overlapping-generations models. *Journal of Public Economics*, 21: 79–92.

Burkhauser, R. (1979). The pension acceptance decision of older workers. *Journal of Human Resources*, 14(1): 63–75.

Burkhauser, R. (1991). An introduction to the German Socio-Economic Panel for English-Speaking Researchers. Mimeo, Syracuse University, Syracuse, NY.

Carmichael, L. (1983). Firm-specific human capital and promotion ladders. *Bell Journal*, 14: 251–258.

Casamatta, G., H. Cremer, and P. Pestieau. (2004). Is there political support for the double burden on prolonged activity? Mimeo.

Casamatta, G., H. Cremer, and P. Pestieau. (2005). Voting on pensions with an endogenous retirement age. *International Tax and Public Finance*, forthcoming.

Coile, C., and J. Gruber. (2000a). *Social Security and Retirement*. NBER Working Paper 7830. Cambridge, MA: National Bureau of Economic Research.

Coile, C., and J. Gruber. (2000b). Social security incentives for retirement. In D. Wise (ed.), *Themes in the Economics of Aging*. (pp. 311–341). Chicago: University of Chicago Press.

Crawford, V. P., and D. M. Lilien. (1981). Social security and the retirement decision. *Quarterly Journal of Economics*, 95: 505–529.

Cremer, H., J.-M. Lozachmeur, and P. Pestieau. (2003). Disability testing and the retirement decision. Unpublished manuscript.

Cremer, H., J.-M. Lozachmeur, and P. Pestieau. (2004a). Optimal retirement and disability benefits with audit. *Finanz Archiv*, 60: 278–295.

Cremer, H., J.-M. Lozachmeur, and P. Pestieau. (2004b). The social desirability of an earnings test. Unpublished manuscript.

Cremer, H., J.-M. Lozachmeur, and P. Pestieau. (2004c). Social security and variable retirement schemes: An optimal income taxation approach. *Journal of Public Economics*, 88: 2259–2282.

Cremer, H., and P. Pestieau. (2003). The double dividend of postponing retirement. *International Tax and Public Finance*, 10: 419–434.

Crepon, B., N. Deniau, and S. Perez-Duarte. (2002). Wages productivity and worker characteristics: A French perspective. Mimeo.

Crepon, B., N. Deniau, and S. Perez-Duarte. (2003). Productivité et salaire des travailleurs âgés. *Revue Française d'Économie*, 18: 157–185.

Dellis, A., R. Desmet, A. Jousten, and S. Perelman. (2004). Micro-modelling of retirement in Belgium. In J. Gruber and D. Wise, eds., *Social Security Programs and Retirement around the World* (pp. 41–98). Chicago: Chicago University Press.

Desmet, R., and A. Jousten. (2004). The decision to retire: Individual heterogeneity and actuarial neutrality. Unpublished manuscript.

Desmet, R., A. Jousten, S. Perelman, and P. Pestieau. (2003). *Microsimulation of social security reforms in Belgium*. Discussion Paper 735. Bonn: IZA.

De Vits, E. (2002). *L'homme et le travail. La vision des jeunes, des actifs et des inactifs*. Brussels: Randstad Belgium.

Diamond, P. (1965). National debt in a neoclassical model. *American Economic Review*, 55: 1126–1150.

Diamond, P. (2002). *Social Security Reforms*. Oxford: Oxford University Press.

Diamond, P. (2003). *Taxation, Incomplete Markets and Social Security*. Cambridge, MA: MIT Press.

Diamond, P., and B. Köszegi. (2003). Quasi-hyperbolic discounting and retirement. *Journal of Public Economics*, 87: 1839–1872.

Diamond, P., and J. Mirrlees. (1978). A model of social insurance with variable retirement. *Journal of Public Economics*, 10: 295–336.

Diamond, P., and J. Mirrlees. (1986). Payroll-tax-financed social insurance with variable retirement. *Scandinavian Journal of Economics*, 88: 25–50.

Diamond, P., and J. Mirrlees. (2004). Social insurance with variable retirement and private saving. Unpublished manuscript.

Diamond, P., and E. Sheshinski. (1995). Economic aspects of optimal disability benefits. *Journal of Public Economics*, 57: 1–13.

Disney, R., and S. Smith. (2002). The labour supply effect of the abolition of the earnings rule for older workers in the United Kingdom. *Economic Journal*, 112: 136–152.

Dohmen, T. (2003). *Performance, seniority and wages: Formal salary systems and individual earnings profiles*. Discussion Paper 935. Bonn: IZA.

Duval, R. (2003). The retirement effects of old-age pension and early retirement schemes in OECD countries. Mimeo, Department of Economics, OECD, Paris.

European Commission. (2003). *Adequate and Sustainable Reforms*. Brussels: European Commission.

Fabel, D. (1994). *The Economics of Pension and Variable Retirement Schemes*. New York: Wiley.

Feldstein, M. (1974). Social security, induced retirement and aggregate capital accumulation. *Journal of Political Economy*, 82: 905–926.

Fenge, R. (1995). Pareto efficiency of the pay-as-you-go pension system with intragenerational fairness. *FinanzArchiv*, 52: 357–363.

Fenge, R., and M. Werding. (2004). Aging and the tax implied in public pension schemes: Simulations for selected OECD countries. *Fiscal Studies*, 25: 159–200.

Fernandez, R., and D. Rodrik. (1991). Resistance to reform: Status quo bias in the presence of individual-specific uncertainty. *American Economic Review*, 81: 1146–1155.

Ferrera, M. (1993). *EC Citizens and Social Protection: Main Results from a Eurobarometer Survey*. Brussels: European Commission, Division V/E/2.

Fields, G., and O. Mitchell. (1984). *Retirement, Pensions and Social Security*. Cambridge, MA: MIT Press.

Flabbi, L., and A. Ichino. (2001). Productivity, seniority and wages: New evidence from personnel data. *Labour Economics*, 8: 359–387.

Friedberg, L. (2000). The labor supply effects of the social security earnings tests. *Review of Economics and Statistics*, 112: 605–637.

Gruber, J., and D. A. Wise. (1999a). *Social Security and Retirement around the World*. Chicago: Chicago University Press.

Gruber, J., and D. A. Wise. (1999b). Social Security and Retirement around the World: Introduction and Summary. In J. Gruber and D. A. Wise, eds., *Social Security and Retirement around the World*. Chicago: Chicago University Press.

Gruber, J., and D. A. Wise. (2002). *Social Security Programs and Retirement around the World: Micro Estimation*. NBER Working Paper 9407. Cambridge, MA: National Bureau of Economic Research.

GSOEP. (2001). *The German Socio-Economic Panel*. Available at ⟨http://www.diw-berlin.de/gsoep⟩.

Hamermesh, D. S. (1986). The demand for labor in the long run. In O. Ashenfelter and R. Layard, eds., *Handbook of Labor Economics* (vol. 1, pp. 429–471). Amsterdam: North-Holland.

Hamermesh, D. S. (1993). *Labor Demand*. Princeton, NJ: Princeton University Press.

Hebbink, G. E. (1993). Production factor substitution and employment by age group. *Economic Modelling*, 10: 217–224.

Hellerstein, J. K., and D. Neumark. (1995). Are earnings profiles steeper than productivity profiles? Evidence from Israeli firm-level data. *Journal of Human Resources*, 30: 89–112.

Hellerstein, J. K., D. Neumark, and K. R. Troska. (1999). Wages, productivity and workers characteristics: Evidence from plant-level production functions and wage equations. *Journal of Labor Economics*, 17: 409–446.

Herbertsson, T., and J. M. Orszag. (2003). *The Early Retirement Burden: Assessing the Costs of the Continued Prevalence of Early Retirement in OECD Countries*. Discussion Paper 816. Bonn: IZA.

Hoegeland, T., and T. J. Klette. (1999). Do higher wages reflect higher productivity? In J. Hattewager et al. ed., *The Creation and Analyse of Employer-Employee Matched Data*. Amsterdam: North-Holland.

Hu, S. C. (1979). Social security, the supply of labor and capital accumulation. *American Economic Review*, 69: 274–284.

Jacobs, L., and R. Shapiro. (1998). Myths and misunderstandings about public opinion toward social security. In R. D. Arnold, M. Graetz, and A. Munnell, eds., *Framing the Social Security Debate: Values, Politics and Economics* (pp. 355–388). Washington, DC: National Academy of Social Insurance.

Kerkhofs, M., M. Lindeboom, and J. Theeuwes. (1999). Retirement, financial incentives and health. *Labour Economics*, 6: 203–227.

Kotlikoff, L. J., and J. Gokhale. (1992). Estimating a firm age productivity profile using the present value of workers' earnings. *Quarterly Journal of Economics*, 107: 1215–1242.

Kotlikoff, L. J., and L. H. Summers. (1979). Tax incidence in a life-cycle model with variable labor supply. *Quarterly Journal of Economics*, 93: 705–718.

Laibson, D. (1997). Golden eggs and hperbolic discounting. *Quarterly Journal of Economics*, 112: 443–477.

Lazear, E. P. (1979). Why is there mandatory retirement? *Journal of Political Economy*, 87: 1261–1269.

Lazear, E. P. (1981). Agency, earnings profiles, and hours restrictions. *American Economic Review*, 71: 606–620.

Lazear, E. P. (1999). Personnel economics: Past lessons and future directions. *Journal of Labor Economics*, 17: 199–236.

Lazear, E. P., and R. L. Moore. (1984). Incentives, productivity, and labor contracts. *Quarterly Journal of Economics*, 99: 275–296.

Lumsdaire, R. L., and D. Mitchell. (1999). New developments in the economic analysis of retirement. In O. Ashenfelter and D. Card, eds., *Handbook of Labor Economics* (vol. 3). Amsterdam: North-Holland.

Marchand, M., P. Pestieau, and M. Racionero. (2003). Optimal redistribution programs when different workers are indistinguishable. *Canadian Journal of Economics*, 36: 911–922.

Michel, P., and P. Pestieau. (2000). Retraite par répartition et âge de la retraite. *Revue Économique* (special issue), 51: 15–30.

Michel, P., and P. Pestieau. (2003). Optimal taxation of capital and labor income with social security and variable retirement age. *FinanzArchiv*, 59: 1–14.

Mitchell, O. S., and P. Levine. (1988). The baby booms's legacy: Relative wages in the twenty-first century. *American Economic Review, Papers and Proceedings*, 78: 66–69.

Mitchell, O., and J. Phillips. (2000). *Retirement Responses to Early Social Security Benefit Reductions*. NBER Working Paper 7963. Cambridge, MA: National Bureau of Economic Research.

Mulligan, C., and X. Sala-i-Martin. (1999). *Gerontocracy, Retirement and Social Security*. NBER Working Paper 7117. Cambridge, MA: National Bureau of Economic Research.

Myers, R. J. (1982). Why do people retire from work early? *Aging and Work*, 5: 83–91.

Myers, R. J. (1983). Further about controversy on early retirement study. *Aging and Work*, 6: 105–109.

O'Donoghue T., and M. Rabin. (1999). Procrastination in preparing for retirement. In H. Aaron, ed., *Behavioral Dimensions of Retirement Economics* (pp. 169–206). Washington, DC: Brookings Institute Press and Russell Sage Foundation.

OECD. (2001). *OECD Labour Market Statistics*. Paris: Organisation for Economic Co-operation and Development.

OECD. (2002). *OECD Economic Outlook*, no. 72. Paris: Organisation for Economic Co-operation and Development.

Oliviera, M. de, E. Cohn, and B. F. Kiker. (1989). Tenure, earnings and productivity. *Oxford Bulletin of Economics and Statistics*, 51: 1–14.

Parsons, D. (1980). The decline of male labor-force participation. *Journal of Political Economy*, 88: 117–134.

Parsons, D. (1982). The male labour force participation decision: Health, reported health and economic incentives. *Economica*, 49(193): 81–91.

Parsons, D. (1991). The health and earnings of rejected disability insurance applicants: Comment. *American Economic Review*, 81: 1419–1426.

Parsons, D. (1996). Imperfect "tagging" in social insurance programs. *Journal of Public Economics*, 62: 183–207.

Quinn, J. F. (1977). Microeconomic determinants of early retirement: A cross-sectional view of white married men. *Journal of Human Ressources*, 12(3): 329–346.

Samuelson, P. A. (1958). An exact consumption-loan model of interest with or without the social contrivance of money. *Journal of Political Economy*, 66: 467–482.

Schokkaert, E., M. Verhue, and G. Peppermans. (1999). Les Flamands et leur système de pension. In *Réflexions sur l'avenir de nos retraites*. Leuven: Garants.

Simonovits, A. (2004). *Modeling Pension Systems*. New York: Palgrave MacMillan.

Statistisches Bundesamt. (2002). *Statistisches Jahrbuch 2002*. Wiesbaden: Statistisches Bundesamt.

Stiglitz, J. E. (1987). Pareto efficient and optimal taxation and the new welfare economics. In A. J. Auerbach and M. Feldstein, eds., *Handbook of Public Economics* (vol. 2, chap. 15). Amsterdam: North-Holland.

Stock, J. H., and D. A. Wise. (1990a). The pension inducement to retire: An option value analysis. In D. A. Wise, ed., *Issues in the Economics of Aging* (pp. 205–224). Chicago: University of Chicago Press.

Stock, J. H., and D. A. Wise. (1990b). Pensions, the option value of work, and retirement. *Econometrica*, 58: 1151–1180.

Verband Deutscher Rentenversicherungsträger (VDR). (1970, 1980, 1990, 2000). *Statistik Rentenzugang des jeweiligen Jahres einschliesslich Rentenwegfall*. Rentenänderung / Änderung des Teilrentenanteils. Frankfurt am Main: VDR.

Verband Deutscher Rentenversicherungsträger (VDR). (2002). *Die Rentenversicherung in Zeitreihen*. Frankfurt am Main: Verband Deutscher Rentenversicherungsträger.

# Index